DOG DAYS

DOG DAYS

Dispatches from Bedlam Farm

———

JON KATZ

VILLARD  NEW YORK

Copyright © 2007 by Jon Katz

All rights reserved.

Published in the United States by Villard Books, an imprint of The Random House Publishing Group, a division of Random House, Inc., New York.

VILLARD and "V" CIRCLED Design are registered trademarks of Random House, Inc.

All photographs by Peter Hanks

Pig barn restoration, pictured on pages iv and 262, done by Bill and Maria Heinrich

Dairy barn restoration, pictured on pages 218 and 268, done by Anthony Armstrong

ISBN 978-1-4000-6404-5

Printed in the United States of America on acid-free paper

www.villard.com

2 4 6 8 9 7 5 3 1

First Edition

Book design by Susan Turner

For Bruce Tracy

(God help me if the stuff he took out had stayed in.)

Animals have always awakened something in me—their little joys and travails alike—that, try as I might, I find impossible to express except in the language of devotion. Maybe it is the Lord's way of getting through to the particularly slow and obstinate, but if you care about animals you must figure out why you care.

—MATTHEW SCULLY,
*Dominion: The Power of Man,
the Suffering of Animals, and the Call to Mercy*

Professor Chernowitz, and other readers:
No dogs die in this book.

DOG DAYS

Dog Days

EACH WINTER HAS A PERSONALITY OF ITS OWN; THIS ONE HAD BEEN gentle in terms of snowfall yet relentlessly cold, with few storms but lots of nasty ice and miserable temperatures. And it was hanging on.

It would be weeks before we could stop putting out hay to feed the animals and rely completely on the pasture, still brown and scrubby on this sunny, chill March morning.

Hay purchases are always something of an annual crapshoot. Buying quality hay that helps your growing population survive and flourish, ordering enough to last through the dark months—it's not simple. During my first winter at Bedlam Farm, a period of general chaos, I'd given the animals two or three times as much as they needed; in the spring, it took weeks to cart away the rotting leftovers. Now my hay was green, moist, and nutritious, and I had learned to smell and squeeze and poke it just like real farmers do. I had ordered five hundred bales this year, and it looked like I might just make it to spring.

This Sunday, the donkeys were by the gate, hoping for cookies. The sheep were lying in a wide ring around the hay feeder, peaceably chewing. I still haven't come to truly love my flock of Tunis, but they do know how to gaze meaningfully at nothing, quietly marking the passage of time.

We were all awaiting one of my favorite rituals, the arrival of a new breeding ram. Rumsfield, the ram from the previous year, was so gentle and affable a fellow that I'd had him neutered and kept him on the farm.

As usual, I'd made up my mind not to breed lambs this year; there was enough going on at my farm, with my dogs, with my life. As usual, I'd changed my mind. Lambing had turned out to be one of the most satisfying parts of life on Bedlam Farm.

My first year, when the lambs were born in mid-February of a brutal winter, was something of a catastrophe, complete with breech births and vaginal prolapses among the flock; frostbite, exhaustion, and panic for me; and dramatic midnight visits from the large-animal vets. Every ewe seemed determined to give birth at three a.m. in howling winds and sub-zero temperatures. If not for my border collie Rose—then just a puppy—who helped me find the newborns in the darkness, kept them with their mothers, helped me lure everyone into the barn and under the heat lamps, I wouldn't have made it, nor would many of the sheep. I was overwhelmed and underprepared, and I lost a couple of my weaker charges.

My second year was easier. I'd learned a lot. Last year's lambs were born later in the spring, with fewer mishaps. I had all the necessary supplies on hand, my lambing pens stood ready, and

I'd overcome any qualms about reaching into ewes to turn or tug at recalcitrant offspring. Turns out I wasn't bad at it, in fact. I only had to call the vet once.

Instead of freezing on successive bitter nights, I sat sipping coffee in a lawn chair on moderate spring days, reading a book and watching the ewes, waiting for Rose to alert me when a lamb was being born.

With her help, the new babies and moms were quickly moved into their pens to rest and recover. I tagged ears and docked tails and administered immunizations, and, after they'd had a few days of the pampered life, sent the sheep out into the world. Lambs, unlike their elders, are curious, playful, inquisitive; it was delightful to see them literally gambol around the pasture.

So why stop now? It seemed a shame not to put my knowledge to use. My cabinets, in both the barn and the kitchen, were still filled with halters, buckets, vitamin supplements, syringes, penicillin, iodine, ear taggers, and tail dockers. Rose and I felt like old hands by now.

So Tunis breeders Wendy and Jim Cameron, who'd sold me my previous two rams, had left their small Massachusetts town at dawn. Around noon, their giant blue Ford truck roared into the driveway, towing a sizable livestock trailer.

The Camerons were in their thirties, warm, friendly, a bit shy, struggling to make their farm work despite higher taxes, increasing governmental regulation, and the rising cost of everything, especially land. We were glad to see each other.

ON A FARM, THERE ARE A NUMBER OF PEOPLE WHO ARE VERY IMPORtant but who you see only once or twice a year—the shearer, the farrier, the farmer who buys my sheep, the folks who sell me firewood and hay, Jim and Wendy. Their visits mark the seasons, milestones in the animals' lives, the rhythms of the farm.

On these occasions, nobody has time for lengthy conversations, or the opportunity or desire to delve deeply into one another's lives. But there's a bond between people who help farms function, a warmth and connection. We're glad to see one another, eager to catch up, to trade stories, gossip, and complaints.

Though I don't make my living farming, I've been largely welcomed into this fellowship. I'd quickly come to understand that nobody can run a farm alone. When you find good, helpful people, you hang on.

The chatter is reassuring. Did you have a good year? How was the winter? What are you paying for hay? Did you lose any animals? Are you making any money?

Because I'm a writer, not a real farmer, my early encounters felt somewhat strained. I couldn't begin to explain to most of these rural craftspeople and farmers that I earned my living writing about dogs.

Now I have battle scars: a sunburned complexion, the hunched crab-walk that marks a farmer, dusty Carhartt sweatshirts, frostbitten fingers. And I'm still more or less standing. So the awkwardness has passed; these visitors are now friends, part of my community.

We grouse about prices, about difficult neighbors, unpredictable weather. We catch up on the lives of our families and kids. Over time, we've come to know many of the same people, so we report deaths and births, successes and failures.

These visitors also show interest in my dogs, and often greet them with biscuits and pats. They're particularly fascinated by my border collie Rose, by far the least social of my dogs but the one they most respect. They've seen her in action. Whereas most people fuss over the sweeter Labs, they understand the worth of a reliable working dog like Rose, a helper, a problem solver.

And we talk animals. Our lives revolve around animals—dogs, sheep, chickens, donkeys, deer, rodents, predators.

Then we do our business, settle up, shake hands, and separate.

Wendy and Jim were among these welcomed seasonal acquaintances. We stood around yakking about sheep, dogs, weather. The Camerons invited me to one of the weekend sheep fairs they frequent, offering me both their home, if I needed a place to stay, and a trailer if I could use one. I reciprocated, offering them the guest room when they were up my way or visiting family in nearby Vermont.

Jim had a gravely ill friend, and I could see how affected he was by it. I'd learned not to stereotype people upstate; the men I met were tough, distracted, frequently tired, but they were also often warm and honest, like Jim, and they often came nose-to-nose with life and death.

How was his friend doing?

"Rough," Jim said, not needing or wanting to add much.

I didn't go into it in detail, but there'd been big changes at Bedlam Farm, too, in the year since I'd last seen these folks. Orson, my beloved border collie, the true instigator of my move to an upstate farm, was gone. I'd been diagnosed with and treated for spinal stenosis, a chronic condition that sometimes brought me low with pain and sometimes limited how much I could move and lift. I had to change some of my routines, to acknowledge that I needed more help running the place.

So I'd hired my friend Annie DiLeo to help me manage the farm and preserve my mobility. Annie loves animals dearly, and has a gift for communicating with them. They were lucky to have her on the case, and so was I.

Aside from my wife and daughter, and the doctors in New York City who helped keep me functioning, I no longer had much connection to my former life in New Jersey. Sometimes, especially in winter, I launched blitzkrieg visits to spend a few days down there with Paula, hitting Thai restaurants and movie theaters, but also contending with traffic, congestion, frayed nerves, bad air, and ghosts of a previous existence. Away from the farm, I was always anxious about it—the animals, the fences, the collapsing barns. It was complicated to leave so many dogs, friends, and responsibilities.

It was easier and more pleasant for Paula, who continued to teach and work in the city, to spend time on the farm, where we'd rehabbed an airy office for her, with a killer view. Our daughter, Emma, living in Brooklyn and working in Manhattan, came up to visit when she could.

For a few weeks after Orson died, I'd had just two dogs, Rose and my Lab Clementine, so indiscriminately loving and agreeable that I called her the Whore of Bedlam Farm. A true Lab—big, stinky, fond of jumping into creeks and rolling in gross stuff—she was the only dog who shared our bed. Paula and I battled her for space and blankets every night. But every morning, when I awoke to her big, beautiful head on my shoulder, I forgave her.

Then there were three. Pearl, the Sad-Eyed Lady of the Lowlands, was also a pale Labrador, a show dog and national champion whom I acquired from a wonderful breeder who relinquished her after she'd injured her legs and could no longer handle the stresses of pregnancy. Pearl was the most loving creature I'd ever encountered; your heart melted when you looked at her. I'd also taken in a new border collie.

But all I told Wendy and Jim was that I'd had some back problems, had lost a dog and gained a couple, and we were doing okay, thanks.

I looked forward to our annual dickering over the ram. Wendy did the negotiating, which, as usual, had begun weeks earlier on the phone.

It was an annual joke. "It'll cost you a bit more this year," she would always say, gravely reciting the rise in gas prices, the cost of grain, the taxes. "I can't help it, the price of things ain't going down." She took pains, too, to point out the titles and lineage of her rams.

She behaved as if she expected an argument—though I never gave her one—and had to justify her price. Three hundred dollars seemed a good price to me. How much money could she make, anyway, on an animal she had raised and fed for several years, then driven two or three hours to deliver to my farm?

"You'll be happy with this guy, he'll do a good job for you," Wendy said as she prepared to unlatch the trailer, our annual catching-up having wound down. "But watch him. He's grumpy. Don't turn your back on him. Don't get hurt." She slipped a halter onto the ram and coaxed him cautiously—he weighed close to three hundred pounds—out the door, through the open gate, and into the pasture.

After a little more discussion, and the nearly ceremonial handover of the check, Wendy and Jim pulled out of the driveway with a farewell honk. I wouldn't see them for another year, most likely.

Rose was in the front yard, watching intently. The farm manager, she kept track of all comings and goings. This newcomer would impact her life dramatically. I knew she would have a lively day, and he would have a long one.

At the moment, he was a dominant and independent creature who believed he was in charge. He'd change his attitude by nightfall.

One of my obsessive pursuits at Bedlam Farm is observing the animals, watching the way the residents here change in relation to one another. The farm is a whole, a collection of its parts, and everything affects everything else. I no longer see this place in terms of sheep or dogs, donkeys, chickens, groundhogs, or coyotes. They are all of a piece, parts of a puzzle.

The ram would almost surely challenge Rose. He would bully the wethers—my neutered male sheep—and the ewes would become more tentative and deferential. His presence would upset the donkeys, who help protect the flock; they'd already moved down to the gate, placing themselves between the sheep and the stranger.

It was Rose's job to sort this out, to whip the ram into shape and wring order from potential chaos.

I'd christened him Rupert in honor of one of my favorite Vermont small towns, just a few miles away. A beautiful place, protected by mountains from much of the development transforming nearby Dorset and Manchester, it was home to a curious mix of Flatlanders much like me, able to buy up and restore old farmsteads, and a band of longtime locals clustered in the center of town.

The men of Rupert were notoriously rich in testosterone. Their backyards were filled with backhoes, tractors, four-wheelers, aging trucks, cannibalized old cars, snowmobiles, and dirt bikes. Some were unhappy—and quite vocal—about the outsiders arriving with ideas about zoning, politics, and guns.

Throughout these beautiful hills, in both Vermont and neighboring New York, you saw this strange, sometimes tense yet symbiotic relationship between the natives and the invading newcomers. The locals often depended on the immigrants for income, since there were few good jobs around. But that didn't mean they had to like them. Animosity often simmered below the surface, sometimes *on* the surface.

My friend Anthony Armstrong grew up in Rupert, and we joked about my idea for a book called *Things Men from Rupert Never Say*. Anthony contributed a few of the items himself.

A sampling:

- "Welcome to Vermont."
- "How would *you* do it?"
- "Sorry, my mistake."
- "I don't know."
- "You're right."

I'd had a few run-ins myself with some of the Rupert grumps, known for strong opinions on everything. It seemed fitting to honor the men of Rupert by naming a ram after them, one its breeder had warned could be belligerent, apt to bump and butt when aroused.

I'd heard such warnings before, but I wasn't terribly concerned. I had Rose.

I let her out of the yard and she trotted up to the pasture gate and lay down. She had that focused, girl-on-a-mission look she wore whenever there was work to do. She hadn't taken her eyes off the livestock trailer from the second Wendy and Jim pulled in.

EVEN FOR A VETERAN LIKE ROSE—ONLY THREE YEARS OLD BUT EX-perienced beyond her years, to the point that farmers sometimes called her for emergency herding—this was a complex situation.

The farm was eerily quiet, every animal still and expectant, reacting to the new arrival, waiting to see what would happen. Animals don't think the way we do, but they certainly know when something is up.

There'd already been some changes and new arrivals on the farm, just in recent days. Watching the drama unfold was a big-eyed baby donkey born unexpectedly two weeks earlier. That made four donkeys arrayed in a defensive line between Rupert and the sheep.

Watching also was Izzy, a gorgeous but anxious three-year-old border collie with a compelling back story. He'd arrived just a few days earlier. Although the plan had been to find him a home—has anyone heard this before?—I was starting to think he might be staying.

So perhaps there were already some disturbances in the field as this large, rambunctious new ram asserted himself. But I was cocky on behalf of my dog.

I opened the gate, stood back, gave no commands. What command was there, anyway, for "avoid-the-donkeys-tame-the-ram-then-go-bring-the-sheep-down-to-me-just-to-show-him-that-you-can"?

Rose entered the pasture, crouched, and gave the intimidating border collie "eye" to everyone in sight.

Without confrontation, she crept up to the donkeys, who retreated to the fence, then locked onto Rupert, who was already sniffing the ewes. Wendy was right: He was focused.

As Rose continued cautiously up the hill, longer-term residents seemed to sense trouble: Mother, the barn cat, popped her head out of the barn, took in the scene, then vanished, and Winston, the rooster, led his hens down the slope and out of harm's way.

When Rose got within about fifteen feet, Rupert finally

took notice. He came thundering toward her, head down. But Rose circled back around the donkeys and came up behind Rupert from the other direction before he could butt, or even turn around. Suddenly charging, she attached herself to his private parts.

The ram gave an odd, short cry and, enraged, tried to attack her. But Rose hung on, pausing now and then to nip his nose, then grabbing him in the rear again. In a few minutes, Rupert was spinning in circles.

After ten minutes of this treatment he retreated into the center of the flock, surrounded by as many ewes as he could possibly put between him and Rose. He stared incredulously at her; she paid him no further mind.

A half hour later, Rupert and the flock were marching dutifully across the road and into the meadow, where, under Rose's watchful eye, they grazed at the first tentative blades of spring grass. Every few moments, Rupert cast a wary eye in Rose's direction. She went into her crouch. He looked away.

SEVERAL HOURS LATER, THE SUN STARTING TO FADE, I LEFT ROSE INside and went out to inspect the barnyard. Rupert was at the hay feeder with the ewes, standing peacefully next to Rumsfield, his good-natured predecessor. Winston, the rooster, was sitting atop the feeder, keeping an imperious eye on everything.

Mother had come out of the barn and was playing a game with the baby donkey, darting back and forth, pawing him harmlessly across the nose. These two had formed an unlikely pair, and even slept together on some still-chilly nights, curled up cozily on a pile of straw in the barn.

The other donkeys, mama Jeannette, plus Lulu and Fanny, were up by the pole barn, taking in the late afternoon sun.

It had been an intense year, equal parts challenge, joy, and grief. I was still adjusting to a life where pain would likely be a continuing element. I was still missing Orson.

And, of course, I was still adjusting to the reality of this strange new existence. None of the things I'd witnessed or been part of today would have been conceivable to me three or four years earlier. Now, it was being without them that had become unimaginable.

Bedlam Farm had turned my life inside out.

A little later, Rose and I went out to usher the donkeys into the barn for the night; it seemed too cold for an infant to stay outside. I slid open the barn door, filled three buckets with grain, and soon felt some warm noses at my butt. The girls needed no further encouragement to come inside.

With the donkeys settled in, I turned on a heat lamp for Winston, still recovering from a mysterious illness some weeks earlier. He and the hens hopped onto their roosts. I gave Mother her evening cat food; she purred, keeping one eye on Rose (these two were not chums) as she wolfed it down. I checked the water buckets, kissed Lulu on the nose, and closed the barn door.

The sheep had marched halfway up the hill and were lying down, clustered for warmth on a cold, windy night. I could see Rupert in the center of the pile, at home amid his harem.

Rose had had a long day and was, for her, weary. Rupert's arrival had created ripples that were confusing, perhaps unsettling. But the farm had worked its way; within just a few hours, the gentle, tranquil feeling I cherished had reestablished itself.

"Good girl, Rosie." I sat as she looked at the sheep, then came over to lick my hand.

The descending calm was satisfying, soothing, and not an accident, I like to think. My philosophy about running this place has evolved, a process that's involved learning about animals, trial and error, arguments, pleas for help, visiting other farms, endless yakking with farmer friends.

Rose and I checked the fences and gates, then headed into the house. I brought the other dogs in from the yard and fed everybody, including myself. Then, with Clem next to me on the sofa, Pearl in front of the woodstove, and Izzy by my feet, I called Paula to see how her day had gone. We were all in for the night.

Carol and Jon

ONE

Carol's Time

ABOUT THAT BABY DONKEY. AS I WAS HEADING DOWN ROUTE 30 A couple of weeks earlier, returning from the hardware store in town, my cell phone warbled. Anthony, working at the farm that day, was calling to say that there was a new donkey in the pasture.

Knowing this had to be a joke, since I had no male donkeys and, to my knowledge, no pregnant ones either, I laughed, fired off some appropriately obscene macho banter—the staple of male conversation hereabouts—and hung up.

It never really crossed my mind that it was true.

When I pulled into the driveway, though, I nearly drove into a fencepost. There was a tiny new donkey, soaking wet from amniotic fluid, hugging close to Jeannette, my most recently acquired Sicilian donkey. The afterbirth was close by and fresh. And Jeannette was snorting like a bull and glowering at any interlopers.

No way, I thought.

Way. Obviously, donkeys have a very long gestation period. Jeannette must have got knocked up just before she arrived last spring. I phoned an SOS to the Granville Large Animal Veterinary Service and ran into the house for some towels.

Jeannette and I are pretty tight, thanks to my daily offerings of carrots, apples, and oat cookies. She let me pick up her newborn—I named her Emma, after my own daughter—dry her off, and make sure her throat and eyes were clear. When I scratched her fuzzy little nose, she closed her eyes and went to sleep in my arms.

I gave Jeannette some cookies for energy, checked to see that she had milk in her teats—she did, a lot of it—and brushed her down a bit to calm her. Then I knelt in front of her and she put her head on my shoulder.

"Congratulations," I said. "Who's the father? You can tell me." But she just went over to Emma and nosed her.

There aren't many donkeys born around here these days. Once, donkeys were the tractors and ATVs of country life, performing agricultural and mercantile tasks integral to farming and commerce. Now they're generally considered useless—local farmers call them "hay suckers"—so they're rare. So people from nearby farms soon began showing up to check out the newcomer, alerted by the mysterious rural news network by which everyone instantly knows everything.

In an hour or so, Kirk the vet showed up, gave the donkeys their appropriate shots, said they were fine. He also told me that Emma was, oops, a male. So "she" became Jesus (using the Spanish pronunciation), thanks to the mysterious circumstances of his birth.

I razzed Kirk about the fact that two large-animal vets had been by in recent weeks and, when I mentioned Jeannette's burgeoning girth, said she'd been eating too much hay and probably had gas.

Truth to tell, I felt guilty about the way I'd been mocking Jeannette for her hearty appetite and swelling belly, never guessing that she was eating for two. Probably she should have had better prenatal care, possibly some supplements. But she'd managed the whole process quite efficiently on her own, it seemed, even selecting an unusually warm February day to give birth.

A cold wave was approaching in forty-eight hours, though, so we scurried to find the heat lamps and bring Jeannette and Jesus into a cozy corner of the barn.

All this made me think even more about why I own donkeys at all.

When I got my troubled border collie Orson, we started learning to herd at a sheep farm in Pennsylvania. A lonely old donkey named Carol lived in the adjacent pasture. We bonded; I was enchanted by her soulful eyes and gentle bray, and she loved the apples I brought her and the pats and scratches that accompanied them. When I bought the farm in upstate New York, I imported some of the sheep we'd been herding with. They arrived on a livestock trailer, and Carol showed up with them, a surprise gift from the farmer, who thought she deserved a better life.

Carol seemed initially stunned, then appreciative of her new life—ample pasture, fresh water, treats and cookies, pats and grooming. But she had some serious health issues. That meant a lot of visits from vets, something Carol didn't appreciate— Amanda, her primary care physician, had to call a half hour before coming, so I could lure Carol into the barn with oats.

Carol could hear Amanda's truck from some distance, and if she could, she'd take off up the hill.

She needed the vets, though. She'd arrived with all sorts of ailments—eye infections, bad circulation, and weak lungs. Our first winter, she'd foundered (foundering is an equine wasting disease of the hoof), and developed sores and abscesses. I'd spent innumerable hours, often in the middle of the night and in freezing temperatures, administering shots, pills, and salves. The veterinary bills, plus the shelves of painkillers, antibiotics, syringes, and thermometers, had run into the thousands.

I think I'd never truly lived until I was called upon to take a rectal thermometer reading from an agitated donkey at five a.m. when the temperature was twenty below.

Carol was agreeable, but not that agreeable. We had many a brawl in the barn and pasture while I attempted to administer her growing list of meds. She wasn't above running, butting, bumping, or dragging me if she spotted a hypodermic.

The nasty case of frostbite that plagues me to this day came one bitter night as she dragged me up the hill to avoid the thermometer.

Paula asked why I hadn't dressed more warmly, but my neighbors just shrug. They understand the logistics of rectal thermometers: It doesn't work with gloves. Generally Carol submitted, not always graciously.

It seems absurd but, over time, I swear she could read my intentions, or perhaps my emotions. If I was simply bringing oats for a treat, Carol came running. If I had an agenda, like an approaching vet's or farrier's appointment, she'd trot out of reach. Carol hadn't survived all her years by being foolish.

But she had a calming quality I found eerily soothing. Every night before bed, Rose and I went out to the barn. I carried a granola bar for myself and a cup of oats for Carol.

Rose—always eager to work but able to grasp the import of certain moments—lay down and hardly moved.

I sat on an old stool while Carol and I—and later Fanny—had our nightly munch-and-crunch. I'd put some music on a boom box I left out there. Carol liked Willie Nelson the most; he seemed to ease her mind.

"You really ought to shoot her," my neighbor, a retired dairy farmer, repeatedly advised. "You'll never get your money back from her." That was surely true. He even offered several times to get his deer rifle and do the deed for me.

Yet I was crazy about Carol, felt lucky to have her, and was determined to give her a more comfortable winter.

About Carol's compadres:

Donkey Number 2 joined her when I got a phone call from a woman who described herself as a "Jewish donkey spiritualist," a term I hadn't heard before and don't expect to hear again. Pat bred donkeys and had studied and written about their symbolic significance, their place in the ancient world, and their profoundly spiritual natures.

Both Jewish and Christian theologies abound with biblical and other references to donkeys, she pointed out. Carol, like all my donkeys, wore a cross on her back, a pattern of dark hair behind the shoulders.

Since donkeys are social sorts, Pat declared, Carol was not only lonely, but was unaware of her "donkeyness." Having lived with sheep all of her life, she probably didn't even know she was a donkey. She needed a companion, Pat said. My wife, already embittered by the vet bills, said she could live with Carol being out of touch with her donkeyness. I couldn't, and so little Fanny soon arrived, and then Lulu, her half sister, who Donkey Number 3.

The Jewish donkey spiritualist was, of course, right

donkeys: They are sweet, accepting, seemingly wise. Min
an ostensible purpose: They're my security detail, fiercely
tective of my flock of sheep. They run off stray dogs and c
otes. And as I've lost no sheep to these common predators, th
donkeys seem to me to be doing their jobs pretty well.

But they also—and this is why I have more donkeys than I
truly need—attach to people. They nuzzle and lean into humans they like, which can sometimes be disconcerting but is
also touching. They are gentle with children, calm around
strangers. They coexist reasonably amiably with my dogs and
chickens, getting irritated only when the hay feeder gets too
crowded.

When I sit out in the pasture, Lulu is usually the first to drift
up behind me and rest her chin on the top of my head, waiting
for her nose to be scratched. The others soon slide alongside,
waiting for pats, carrots, scratches. We sit in this odd, cuddly
huddle for long periods sometimes, especially when I need
soothing or company. Their silent affection is quite potent, if
you wait for it.

Donkeys are always watching and miss little. Nothing seems
to surprise them, or seems new to them. My private theory is
that some of the wisdom of the ages has been passed along in
their genes, and a little may rub off on me, if I allow it.

When I come out of the house in the morning, the girls
(and now Jesus, too) are waiting for me at the barnyard gate,
wheezily braying for their cookies. Serious about snacks,
they're apt to nose into your pockets if you're slow to produce
them.

But our connection goes well beyond food. Apart from the
cuddling and brushing, I often go check on them at night before I go to sleep. During winter storms, I trudge up to the pole

barn and comb ice from their long eyelashes; they hold still for
the procedure, then nuzzle me in appreciation.

LAST YEAR, DONKEY SPIRITUALIST PAT SOLD HER FARM. BEFORE SHE
moved away, she sold me Jeannette, one of her oldest donkeys
(they live to be thirty, even forty). Nobody said anything about
anybody being pregnant. But Jeannette was, apparently.

So now there were four. "That's a lot of hay," one of my in-
credulous farmer neighbors observed. "Especially for animals
that don't do anything."

He's wrong; they do a lot for me. They connect me to nature and history. They're dutiful watchdonkeys, affectionate
companions. In many ways, they are the soul of my farm. I want
to do well by them.

ONE OF THE MANY SECOND-YEAR INNOVATIONS AT THE FARM,
therefore, was the Donkey Motel, a corner of the barn where
Anthony had installed insulation, wiring for heat lamps, and a
small hay feeder. The younger donkeys were hearty creatures,
but Carol had suffered grievously from the cold the first winter; she'd need more protection.

After all those lonely years by herself in the woods, she
seemed entitled to a few easy ones on my farm. Anthony carefully sealed the cracks in the barn so the Donkey Motel would
be sound.

He appreciated her, even if he doubted my sanity for spending money on her. Anthony's daughter, Ida, who was then two,
liked to crawl beneath Carol's legs, which didn't bother Carol
at all; she merely nuzzled Ida with her nose. Once, I was horri-

fied to look up and see Ida and Carol munching on opposite ends of the same carrot. Anthony often said there was no safer place for his daughter than underneath that donkey.

So that fall, when the farmer's weather alert service—I loved merely being on the list—called to advise that winter was arriving suddenly and brutally, I felt prepared.

Temperatures would drop from the forties into the single digits overnight, and high winds would drive the windchill well below zero, the service advised. "Winter is coming," somebody said at the Bedlam's Corner Variety Store down the hill, "with a bite." But Carol would be safe in her motel.

When I lived in Boston or Philadelphia or New Jersey, I couldn't understand the big deal local newscasters made of weather forecasts. I looked out the window in the morning and either wore a raincoat or parka, or didn't.

But at Bedlam Farm, I pay acute attention. Weather isn't just about what to wear, although that matters, but about livestock: hay supplies, feed and corn, deicers and water flow, shelter from the wind and wet. Most farm animals can handle all but the most brutal cold, but not my aging donkey.

It had been evident all that summer that Carol was no longer hardy. She moved less, hugged the barn more, and as the fall chill came, she seemed weary, reserving her energy for the advancing winter.

When it comes to animals, it's easy to anthropomorphize, attributing human emotions and thoughts to other species. I'm certain that Carol had little sense of herself as tired or vulnerable, just as she probably had no concept of herself as "lonely." She'd survived for many years on her own, without the hay and snacks I kept bringing. I would have been lonely and uncomfortable in her previous existence, but for all I know, she was content with her hideaway.

To my mind, Carol had anchored that first chaotic, over-whelming year at Bedlam Farm, for which I was immensely grateful. She projected confidence and calm; she was so unflappable that she steadied me. She just made me feel better.

And not only me. Kids from miles around came to see her and bring her carrots, and she greeted them all warmly and patiently, even when they shrieked or pulled cookies right out of her mouth.

She appeared out of the mist or snow whenever I emerged from the house. She hovered over the birth of each lamb. I thought of her as the silent but faithful witness to this strange journey I'd taken with my dogs and my restless self.

When I grew confused, frightened, or overburdened—which was a substantial part of the time—I could count on her affection. The one thing, apparently the only thing, she couldn't handle was the cold. This year I thought I could spare her its worst effects.

I wasn't the only one concerned about her. In October, Ken Norman, the farrier from Pawlet, Vermont, came to trim the donkeys' hooves. He drove a converted red fire truck stocked with medieval-looking tools. In his leather apron, he handled the donkeys with a particular ease and authority. Even Carol submitted calmly to his trimming and filing. As he worked, he talked quietly to "the girls."

He didn't like the way Carol looked. "She's wearing out," he told me. As skilled as the large-animal vets were, I'd learned, nobody could read a donkey better than a farrier like Ken. It was still golden fall then, fairly warm, but I feared he was right. It had happened gradually, with nothing you could really put your finger on. Carol just seemed to do less of everything—explore, eat, leave the barn. Despite my preparations, I began to wonder.

I e-mailed Pat, the spiritualist, saying I was worried about Carol and pondering how much more medical treatment to subject her to, should further problems arise.

As I'd come to know Pat I'd stopped laughing at the idea of a donkey mystic. If you ever saw her with a donkey, you'd know she does have some way of communicating with them that most of us lack.

My view of animals, my sense of responsibility, was narcissistic, in a way. I often thought it was up to me to make everything okay for them. Not so, Pat warned.

"The decisions are not yours to make about Carol," she said in her reply. "They are her decisions and they will be made by her. Oh, you might well be burdened by the phone call, the visit by the vets, the payment for the needle. But I truly believe that the timing of all deaths is a personal one. . . .

"Death is always on time. In the face of such awesomeness, one cannot dare to speak of monies spent, time wasted, effort expanded. When the time comes, you will do your fated duty and she will go to join the ancestors. Loss, a terrible one, but blessings, in great measure. You were blessed, and all on your farm, by her presence, and she was too, by yours. Perhaps she was waiting for Fanny. And now she can depart in peace. And she will, and you will know it."

Struck by that message, I printed it out and folded it away. I suspected I might need to read it again before the winter was over.

WHEN THE WEATHER ALERT CAME, I WENT OUT TO THE BARN TO BE sure Carol's winter quarters were ready: the floor mucked, the straw bedding piled up, three leaves of hay in the feeder. When

I switched on the heat lamps, the red glow from the Donkey Motel could be seen across the farm.

The cold front hit about nine that night. An icy rain had begun—my least favorite weather. From inside the house I could feel the temperature plummet, hear the windows rattle; the remaining brown leaves whipped off the tree limbs and flew about. I stuffed logs into the woodstove and lit it. The thermometer by the back window, which had read forty degrees just a half hour ago, soon hit fifteen. Welcome to winter.

Rose and I went out to escort Carol to her haven. We make a final check every night. With a powerful torchlight, I sweep the meadow until I've located all the sheep and donkeys. Sometimes I see coyotes skittering along the fence line, or other animals' eyes in the woods. That's normal. But when something is wrong—a sheep is sick or entangled in fencing—Rose seems to know.

This night, she had an alarmed, things-are-not-quite-right look, staring up into the pasture in the border collie crouch. The icy rain was so impenetrable that I couldn't see anything, so I opened the gate and Rose dashed up the hill and out of sight as I picked my way up a slope growing more slippery by the second.

I always appreciated Rose, but all the more so lately because of my bad back. She compensates for that, as for so many things.

Halfway up, I saw Rose circling a donkey, and I soon saw that it was Carol, behaving strangely. Animals can tell you when something is off. Masters of tradition, creatures of habit, their lives revolve around food, shelter, water, sex, and safety. When they change their habits, therefore, you pay attention.

My usually predictable donkey, who never walked the pasture at night, was wandering in circles, seeming not to see or hear me as I called to her. She almost walked into the wall of the pole barn. She appeared confused, as if she'd lost her bearings or perhaps her sight. I scurried off to the barn to get a halter, then struggled back up the hill, wishing I'd brought a cell phone.

As I got close, Carol seemed to notice me for the first time. Her ears were laid back; she looked bewildered. I came up and talked to her—"Hey, girl, what's up? You okay?" I took a donkey cookie, her favorite kind, from my pocket, but she turned away.

Nudging gently, I got her moving. Her head swung back and forth at a strange angle, but she followed me down the slope and into the barn, where I dried her with a towel, guided her into the motel, turned on the heat lamps. It was her first time in the enclosure, but she needed no convincing to stay; she lay down on the straw and sighed, but still wouldn't take a cookie. I sat down next to her, Rose watching from a corner, and stroked her head and nose. At least she would be warm and dry this miserable night.

Back inside the house, I called the vets and left a message asking somebody to come first thing in the morning. Next day, when I let Carol out of the barn, she walked slowly back up the hill, almost precisely to the spot where I'd found her wandering the night before.

Just after breakfast, Dr. Kirk Ayling pulled into the driveway in his white truck and walked up into the pasture. I admire the large-animal vets. They work day and night in all sorts of brutal weather and sometimes impossible conditions. Kirk and I had already been through some strange moments together, from castrating a ram to pulling lambs out of ewes. Now I saw him climb up to Carol, check her heart and pulse, take her temperature. Rose and I walked up to join him.

Kirk dealt mostly in what vets call "production medicine," with farmers whose animals are commodities, who don't have the money or inclination to spend more on an animal's care than it can fetch at market. But he'd also worked with newcomers to the area like me, whose animals were somewhere between products and pets.

Carol was definitely ailing, he told me. Her heart rate was very high. She appeared disoriented. He thought she might have had a stroke.

Even in that first year on the farm, my views about animals had evolved. I had a more holistic sense of farm life, for example—greater reservations about keeping unhealthy animals around, more realistic expectations about healing them, a keener sense of running a well-organized, healthy operation. The farm had become an idea bigger than its parts.

Nothing made me prouder than when another farmer or a vet came by and noticed that I "kept a good, clean barn," or praised my farm. But that sometimes meant making difficult decisions.

Kirk looked at me. "What do you want to do?"

"What do you think?" I responded.

"I think she's had a stroke and she's suffering," he said. "There isn't that much I can recommend to help her. There are things we can try, if you want, but I don't know how effective they would be. It's really up to you. If you're comfortable with it, you might consider putting her down."

"Put her down," I said.

He nodded, watching me, trying to figure out where I stood.

"Do you want to go inside the house?" he asked.

"No," I said.

"Do you need some time alone with her first?"

"Nope."

"Do you want to call a friend or somebody?"

I sighed. "Kirk, let's just do it," I said.

A year earlier, I would have thought it merciful to treat Carol, to have Kirk prescribe a raft of medicines for her and make half a dozen return visits. Because I loved her, I would have put up a fight to prolong her life. But that, I'd come to believe, could be a self-serving notion of mercy.

I had different notions of animal care now. The animals on a functioning farm needed to be healthy; when they weren't, I had priorities to set, choices about how much to spend on which animal for what reason.

If I was really thinking of Carol, I would, as Pat had suggested, pay more attention to her than to me. And after some time on the farm, I knew what Pat meant about all decisions not being up to us. Carol couldn't consciously decide to live or die, or to tell me her wishes, but that didn't mean she couldn't let me know how she was faring. She *was* telling me; what I had to do was listen.

It was too bad she couldn't have enjoyed more of the good life. It was also great that she'd had a chunk of it. She had given me much, but also suffered much. She did seem to me to be letting go; it was obvious in her acquiescence to Kirk's probing and prodding. Her very passivity—she would normally have trotted to the top of the hill at the mere sound of his truck—told me how sick she was.

Did she really need to endure another harsh, long winter so that I could feel heroic? Was that truly compassion? I thought of the great year we'd had together, the nights in the barn, the rain of cookies and oats, the shelter and companionship, equine and human. She'd had a good end-of-life, and I'd done my part.

I faced a sad decision, but not a difficult one. Let her join the ancestors.

"Look, I'm okay," I told Kirk. "I can handle it. Let's just do it."

"Do you want to dig a hole for her body? Or I can have somebody come for a hundred bucks and pick it up. But it won't be like New Jersey," he cautioned.

"I don't live in New Jersey anymore," I assured him.

Clear now about what I wanted, Kirk headed back to his truck for his needles. We agreed to walk Carol down to the pasture gate, where he would administer the injection. Then he would call a rendering company to come the next morning.

Carol followed me down, something she normally would not have done with a vet waiting below. At the gate, she stopped, waited.

I gave Carol a hug and a kiss on her fuzzy nose, and held her head in my arms. Kirk knelt down by her side to administer a dose of sedative, powerful enough to literally stop her heart. For a second I considered whether I should give the injection but, less experienced than he, I feared I might mess it up or prolong the process.

Kirk found the proper spot in her neck and slid the needle in. Carol sighed, looked up at me, then fell to her knees and over onto her side, her eyes closed. "It's done," Kirk said, feeling for her pulse. It was strange to see her lie so still.

"You okay?" he asked. I nodded.

Rose came over to her body and sniffed it. Kirk and I shook hands, and he left.

I sat beside Carol for a little while. Lulu and Fanny came down from the upper pasture. Pat had said it was important that

they see that Carol had died; otherwise they might keep looking for her. So each came over slowly, sniffed a few times, then
backed away.

I felt glad she didn't end her life in a patch of dank woods,
glad nobody called her Carol the Lonely Donkey any longer.

Then I went to haul some hay out for the sheep, and Fanny
and Lulu plodded back up behind the pole barn, nibbling at the
last of the grass before the snow buried it for months.

THE NEXT MORNING, A GRIZZLED, GAP-TOOTHED MAN IN JEANS AND
a T-shirt hopped out of his battered white pickup. The truck
had a pungent odor.

"Hey there," he said cheerfully "Looks like the sheep business is doing good."

"Oh?" I said. "Why's that?"

He looked over at Rose. "Well, that ain't no pound dog," he
said. "You must be making some money."

He offered his hand. "They call me 3-D," he said. "Dead,
Down, and Disabled."

As he chattered, he opened the rear door of his truck. Three
dead cows were piled in the back. He lowered a hydraulic
winch, uncoiled a steel chain, and looped it around Carol's
neck.

"In the summer I'd a been here right away," he said. "But
with the cool weather, I stopped to pick up these cows first.
This one could wait."

He had a lot of stops, 3-D announced cheerfully. Business
was good. Back in the day, he said, dairy farmers only had thirty
or forty cows, and most lived long lives. "But now, some of 'em
got eight and nine hundred head, and if they lose two or three

a week, they don't really care. I'm busy. I work every day of the year," he said.

And he loved his job. "Something different every day," he said, hitting the winch. I stepped aside as Carol's inert body was hauled rapidly up into the truck and atop the cows. 3-D did not ask if I needed a moment alone with her.

"Once in a while," he confided, "they aren't completely dead, so I carry a pistol to finish it off, so they don't suffer."

It both pleased and slightly alarmed me that he didn't ask if I wanted to go into the house.

He also invited me to ride along with him some morning. A versatile professional, he handled chickens, goats, sheep—and dogs too, in case I ever had to shoot or put any down.

"Anything you got to kill, I can take," he said, closing up the truck. The vet would bill me directly, he said cheerfully, as his truck roared and rattled off. I smiled for days afterward thinking of him.

I had no regrets about bringing Carol to the farm or spending so much money to keep her content and comfortable. It had benefited me as much as her, which was fair.

Now I had no regrets, either, about stopping her heart and having 3-D haul her off.

I was not like my farmer friends and neighbors, most of whom would never have kept a donkey at all, nor was I my former self, mourning and brooding over the loss of an animal, cremating its remains, providing some sort of ritual send-off.

Some of the hardheaded farmers nearby might never have the pleasure of seeing an affectionate donkey waiting at the gate every morning; the people who treated their animals like children might not know the satisfaction of learning and keeping perspective. I was still working to figure out my own view of animals and of humans' emotional responses to them, but I knew this much: Carol had done well by me, and I had done right by her.

Yet for many days thereafter when I walked out into the gray chill in the morning, I looked for her by the gate and felt an emptiness because she wasn't there.

IT WAS ENTIRELY FITTING THAT THE MOTEL, ORIGINALLY ENVISIONED as a protective nook for my oldest donkey, was serving now as a maternity ward and nursery for the two newest. Jesus was adorable, with downy gray fur, a pouf of black bangs over his forehead, and eyes that seemed to take up half his face.

But I already had a lot of animals to care for, and four donkeys could tip the scale. I hadn't planned on him, the farm didn't require him, and I was trying to be conscientious about not adding animals simply for the sake of rescuing them or for the temporary pleasure of acquiring something new.

ONCE I GOT OVER THE SHOCK, I WAS CHARMED BY JESUS, WHO FOL-lowed me around like a puppy, at least so far as Jeannette would allow. But I didn't need four donkeys. Nobody needs four donkeys.

I began contacting friends who might want a donkey, once Jesus was older and weaned, or two if I kept mother and son together. I visited several possible homes and farms, rejecting one because it had no fences, another because its residents were rarely there—they lived in New York City and had a caretaker come by once or twice a day.

One potential adopter, a neighbor with twenty acres just down the road, loved Jesus and visited him daily. She was prepared to build him a small shed just beyond her kitchen window. So I agreed to send him over when he was a bit older.

Then one morning, I looked out my own kitchen window to see Jesus, Lulu, and Fanny cantering around the pasture in widening circles, braying and kicking, almost as if they were playing tag. Jeannette was being the den mother, watchful but avoiding the foolishness herself. When I came out to the gate, everyone rushed down for a cookie, and Jesus was the first one there. I scratched his velvety ears.

Mother the cat appeared out of nowhere, as was her wont, and was batting Jesus clawlessly on the nose while he danced around. One of the older ewes—Number 57—had taken a keen maternal interest in him, too. Lulu and Fanny had become quite auntlike, nuzzling and playing with him. Even the businesslike Rose spared him her usual intimidation tactics.

Jesus, I realized, had become the farm mascot. He'd forged a lot of connections in just a couple of weeks. Other animals had taken him in. I felt a pretty strong connection to him myself. And my helper, Annie, had taught him to accept a halter, to love being brushed, and to know his name.

So I had to apologetically call my friend and tell her I'd changed my mind; I would be keeping Jesus on the farm for the foreseeable future. She said she figured. I called Paula ("Big news," she said) and told Anthony ("No kidding") and my daughter, Emma ("There's a shock").

Why, I asked Jeannette, am I so often the last to know?

TWO

———

Heavenly City

ONE OF THE FARM'S TRADITIONS—IF A THREE-YEAR-OLD ENTERPRISE can have traditions—is taking the sheep down to the meadow across from West Hebron's big brick Presbyterian church as services conclude on Easter Sunday. It happened almost by accident the first year: I was startled to look down the hill and see a score of worshipers, all dressed to the nines, gathered in a cluster to watch Rose, then just a puppy, herd the sheep.

Now I run into people all year who ask if Rose and I will take the sheep out on Easter Sunday. Kids remember things like that, and some look forward to it, are growing up with it. So we do.

But before we set off, I read a bit of Augustine's *City of God* to my dogs. I first read it to Orson when we moved upstate, a sort of consecration and dedication for our new farm and the animals taking up residence there.

Paula is often tied up in New York in April; Anthony is not much interested in hearing from Saint Augustine; my Christian friends are in church. It would be obnoxious to impose this impenetrable treatise on anybody else. So the reading usually involves just me and the dogs.

I'm not a religious man, but I respect religious holidays, even envy them in some ways. And I'm conscious of the role faith plays in my life. The late Trappist monk and author Thomas Merton was right, I think, when he said that a meaningful life is not possible without it.

Augustine's writings, which became the foundation for much of modern Christendom, are complex, but at the heart of *City of God* is the notion of two cities spawned at the beginning of the world, one earthly, one heavenly.

The Earthly City is often divided against itself by wars and quarrels, with victories that often prove either short-lived or meaningless. But the Heavenly City is a place of peace and light, "the one that lifts up its head in its own glory. Princes and subjects serve one another in love, faith and conscience." One is the place where we live, in other words, and the other the place we yearn to live.

When I look at the chicken manure, collapsing barns, and rusting fences of Bedlam Farm, I don't want to push comparisons with a Heavenly City too far. Yet it has been a place of peace and light for me, for all its flaws, decay, and continuing jolts of reality.

Much hereabouts had changed since that first reading. Orson was gone, and so was Carol the Once Lonely Donkey. But other dogs and donkeys had joined our little tribe.

Our first winter, as I struggled to navigate the cold and the ice, to feed and water animals, and deliver lambs on sub-zero nights, I wasn't sure I would make it. At the cost of a disintegrating spine, some frostbitten fingers, and many hard-won lessons about the true nature of farms, animals, and the seasons, I had survived.

Now I had more help, cared well for my animals, and was closing in on what would likely be one of the last great dreams of my life: the restoration of this lovely place. The house had been painted a deep and dignified gray; a new stone wall that looked old had risen behind it. Its living room and a family room had been painstakingly restored. The gardens had expanded; an old barn, stripped to its beams and floor, was slowly being rebuilt.

The grandson of Russian immigrants who spent their entire American lives in two rooms, I was privileged to own this farm and I intended to do right by it.

If other people also got to enjoy some of my undertakings and my animals, on a sunny spring Sunday when people think and talk about rebirth, all the better.

EASTER WAS A CRISP, MOSTLY SUNNY, AND VERY BEAUTIFUL DAY THIS spring. The songbirds had arrived in force. A strong southwesterly wind whistled noisily through newly budding trees.

The donkeys and sheep were leaving hay in the feeder to munch on sprouting grass—the true sign of spring.

Yet the day was not proving as serene as I'd hoped. The Labs had found some dead thing the evening before, apparently, and whatever it was had taken a toll on their digestive systems. I awoke to a dreadful mess, which required nearly an entire roll of paper towels and a pint of Odor-Off to clean up. The washer and dryer were in their third cycle.

Lulu was limping, so I got out the hoofpick, knelt down next to her, and pulled a shard of rock out of her hoof. Thus distracted, I didn't notice the new ram, Rupert, scuttle up behind me and butt me. It wasn't too hard a blow, and Rose was on him in a flash and backed him right up, but lightning bolts shot up and down my vulnerable spine.

The water hose had sprung a leak and needed to be patched.

I felt a bit melancholic anyway, as I sometimes do on holidays, when my friends around town are with their families and I am away from my own.

For this morning, then, the dogs would have to serve as my family, for better or worse. How I loved these four. The sad-eyed Pearl had stolen my heart; Rose was my hero; Izzy was proving to be a charmer; Clementine was the happiest dog I had ever known.

I got ready to take the sheep down toward the church; the organ chords wafting up the hill were a signal that the service was under way.

With multiple dogs, you have to make choices about who goes where. Clem knew how to chill, and settled contentedly into her crate. Izzy, the newcomer, was not yet reliable around sheep. Rose was coming, of course, and I wanted Pearl as well.

I've never encountered a more viscerally loving and nurturing dog. A veteran of multiple surgeries, her rear legs held together with titanium screws and nylon thread, Pearl has known much pain in her life, and still does. Yet she loved to come along on excursions, appealing to me with those enormous sad eyes every time I went out.

Pearl couldn't handle long junkets like the other dogs; even lifting her solid seventy-pound frame into the car—because she couldn't jump up into it—was a challenge for my back.

But this trip was just across the road. So I put on a fleece vest and headed out with Pearl and Rose.

EASTER, AND SUNSHINE, WERE VERY WELCOME. THE MONTH BEFORE, mud season had descended on the farm. The spring thaw had begun, but often it lasted only until dusk, when temperatures still plunged below freezing and stretches of black ice coated the roads. The constant melting and thawing, along with the runoff from snowy hills, had turned the place into a bog.

There was nothing heavenly about mud season. Only farms—and maybe zoos—know that rich brew of mud, manure, hay, wet fur, and fleece.

I kept mud shoes and boots by the back door. Every trip outside involved many minutes of pulling shoes on and off, followed by scraping on the return trip. But no matter how much scraping I did, the house grew gamy. The dogs, dark with muck, had to go into their crates to dry off. Even when dry, they were pungent. Soon, smells hung over the living room like wood smoke after a slow fire.

Sometimes I thought the whole farm would simply vanish into a giant smelly sinkhole.

The animals reacted instinctively, adapting and reorganizing themselves to cope with change or discomfort. They had their own customs and routines when it came to foul weather, their own notions of order. This, I often thought, was one of their gifts to us, this ability to live together so patiently and synergistically.

When it rained, the sheep huddled together on one side of

the three-walled pole barn, where they would remain in an almost vegetative state through the night, snug in a tight and highly efficient circle, lending one another warmth and comfort. The donkeys grouped themselves on the other side.

Repelled by wetness and muck, their normal roost disturbed by the barn renovation in progress, Winston the rooster and his three hens often joined them, forming an imperious row atop the hay in the feeder, squawking to one another in complaint. The only moments of discord came when a foolish hen got between Jeannette and the hay, whereupon the hen came flying out of the barn as if fired from a slingshot. Jeannette was generally good-natured, but impatient with anything that interfered with eating, wielding her nose like a nightstick.

Mother halted her murderous rodent patrols and found a bale of straw to doze on up in the hayloft. She liked the warmth of all the animals gathered there.

Sometimes I fantasized that the animals exchanged tips and stratagems for coping with extreme weather, passing predators, and other threats. Inclement weather—take up your stations. Clump together for warmth and safety; conserve your energy; wait it out.

But they had no need for communiqués; the clustering response was embedded in their genes. It was humans who complained and worried and were unprepared, unaccepting. For the animals, mud season was just unpleasantness, nothing to fuss about.

Still, I was struck by the fact that the animals could all squeeze into the small shed—the pole barn measured just twelve by thirty feet—and keep one another warm through the night without quarreling, struggling for position, or fighting over hay.

I liked to see it. The farm was, at times, becoming a serene place. And I was working hard and continuously to make it so.

TRYING TO ASSEMBLE A SORT-OF-HEAVENLY CITY IN WEST HEBRON is not a casual thing.

I choose these animals with care, visiting and observing them, approaching them, asking their owners and breeders about their lineage, health, and temperament. I feed them early in the morning when they're hungry, then again at night, and I give them good, fresh, nutritious stuff. There's always fresh water around, and everybody has room to maneuver. I quickly tend to pain or discomfort. There's shelter at hand from the wind, rain, snow, or bitter cold.

The idea is to make them comfortable, settle them into familiar routines, give them what they need.

I've grown ruthless about defending the farm. I've used a gun, when necessary, to keep predators at bay. I've also used it to deal quickly with seriously ill animals the vets couldn't restore to health. I want a healthy, functioning farm, not a rescue clinic.

The responsibility of caring for these animals mercifully and well humbles me. I don't believe animals think the way we do, but they do seem to know when they are loved and safe.

I was learning firsthand that if I gave the animals what they needed, they'd have little reason to be obnoxious, competitive, or aggressive. They would settle into comfortable routines, at ease with me and with one another. Thus other people would be at ease with them, too. The wheel would keep turning; the kingdom would stay peaceable.

Take food, for example. Donkeys and sheep and dogs obviously need calories, but food isn't just nourishment to them. It's what their lives tend to revolve around, finding it and eating it.

When I get a new dog or donkey or ewe, I always approach it with food, at least for the first few months. My sweatshirt pockets are stuffed with donkey cookies, dog biscuits, apples, and carrots. Whenever the newcomer sees me, I'm bearing gifts. I become synonymous with sustenance and survival, and animals come to see my arrival as a happy and nourishing event. Once this view has taken hold, I can ease up, keep fewer provisions crammed into my pockets. I'm already good news.

This all comes easier for me than for real farmers, of course. I don't have to milk cows, grow potatoes or alfalfa, or make organic goat cheese to truck to Manhattan restaurants. I don't need to turn a profit by raising or selling livestock, a very hard job in the best of times—and these are not, for local farmers, very good times at all.

I can afford vet care, quality hay, good fences. I can keep donkeys because I love them. I can hire people to help me haul around the things they need.

Yet Bedlam Farm is also, in some ways, a true farm. Animals live and reproduce here. Fleece and manure are sold; sheep are sent to market. I have three busy dogs to feed, exercise, train, and love.

This sprawling, hilly place has to be managed. I have to buy hay, collect eggs, move sheep, supervise feeding and breeding and shoeing and shearing. Someone has to be found to haul off felled trees, dig drainage ditches, brush-hog overgrown fields, mend fences, and maintain the grounds and gardens. I oversee projects to restore collapsing buildings and barns.

I write about my animals, and so, in a way, they are my crop; they do provide my living.

If the farm renews me, it also sometimes wears me out with its constant cycle of health and sickness, disruption and repair, life and death.

People tell me all the time that I'm living out their fantasies, but when I take stock of my blistered and stiffened hands, my painful back and sore legs, and all the chores and tasks I can never catch up with, I wonder if they would really want to trade places. No place is perfect, no life without conflict, travail, or immunity to the tolls of late middle age.

Much of the time, nonetheless, I feel almost superstitious about having a place I cherish so much, and distinctly unworthy. What have I done to deserve such a haven?

Every day is a decision, and I choose to be here, until the day comes when, as Augustine believed, I will leave my animal body and live in peace and without want.

ROSE MARCHED THE SHEEP DOWN INTO THE CENTER OF THE NEWLY green meadow. Spring had arrived nearly overnight and the sun and wind had already dried much of the mud and the muck. We had about a half hour, I calculated, before services ended.

"Rose, hold them," I said, instructing her to lie down with the flock and be still for a while. This command sometimes worked and sometimes didn't. Rose had a distinct picture in her head of where sheep ought to be, but she hadn't made me a copy, so I was at a disadvantage. No matter what commands I gave, if the flock moved too far or in the wrong direction, she got up and put them where she thought appropriate. Then she would lie down and stay.

This was a fair deal, to my mind. These were very much Rose's sheep. They trusted her, followed her, grazed right next to her. I was merely the shepherd accompanying them on a walk.

Rose liked the sheep where they were, apparently, and lay nearby, watching for any aberrant or unauthorized behavior. When she was working, Rose did not take treats, seek or give affection, succumb to distractions, or lose sight of the mission. That left me free to daydream, listen to the hymns, and scratch Pearl's belly. I lowered myself slowly onto a rock—and Pearl did her job, which was to collapse onto my lap. I hugged her and kissed her nose.

As we waited for the churchgoers to emerge, I thought of Orson, who'd been with me the previous Easter. I felt both grateful and sorrowful for Pearl, and for all her great and innocent heart had endured, and would endure: It was likely she would not live a long life, or one free of pain. I wished for hope and renewal for my friends and my far-flung family.

Then the organ music swelled and people began streaming out of the church toward their cars. Soon, a gaggle of kids was standing at the edge of the parking lot, looking across a creek too wide to cross with sheep in early spring.

"Hey, Rose!" they yelled. Everyone in town seemed to know her name.

I squeezed Pearl and got to my feet, a wordless signal for Rose to get to work, marching the sheep up and down the meadow. These people didn't stand in the church lot to see an aging man sitting on his butt, cuddling his Labrador.

I hoped all the same gentle creatures would be here on the farm the next Easter. But I accepted that some of them would almost surely not be, that some of us would move from the earthly realm to the other one.

Augustine probably had a different place in mind, perhaps a place a bit less pungent, with fewer curious, energetic, and slobbering dogs. But as the sheep grazed under Rose's watchful care and Pearl took in the view and I turned to look back at my patched-together homestead shimmering in the sunlight, I thought it qualified.

Izzy

THREE

Izzy

At first I just listened to the phone message a couple of times. I wasn't sure I should call back.

I'm fond of Amy, a rescue person, but she also makes me a bit nervous. I'm wary of the emotional intensity surrounding animal rescue and some of the people who do it.

Amy regularly calls my farm, and others, seeking homes for animals in trouble. They might be donkeys retiring from duty in national parks, abused goats from Buffalo, cats, rabbits, and dogs, of course.

Sometimes—I've told Amy this—I worry that the desire to rescue can become an unceasing cycle. There's no end to the need. If you love animals—any animals—you will sooner or later become acquainted with their suffering. Amy's small farm along the Vermont border is already crammed with animal refugees she's taken in.

I think what makes me uncomfortable is that under different circumstances, I could probably become Amy. Or my sister, who shares a small house and yard some hours west of here with rescue dogs (eight ailing Newfoundlands with heart disease, at this juncture, plus some dogs in foster care), donkeys, ducks, goats, a horse, chickens—the cast of characters changes often.

I don't want the rescue impulse to dominate or overwhelm me; it could, I know, swallow me up. Yet I am drawn to it. So Amy understands, when she leaves messages, that sometimes I return the calls, sometimes I don't. I understand why she keeps trying: She sees my place as a beautiful haven that could shelter a lot of animals in trouble. But while I've helped Amy place donkeys, dogs, and horses, she hasn't placed any with me.

Still, rescue people are often determined advocates who fight hard. When an animal and a human connect, when the match feels perfect, they like to say the dog or cat or horse has "hit the jackpot." It's pure joy for them to see, the thing they most aspire to. So Amy had learned to be wily.

"Hey, Jon, this is Amy," said the message that arrived late on a dark March afternoon. "Listen, I have a couple of donkeys from the U.S. Bureau of Land Management out west who need homes." (They take tourists on rides up difficult trails.) "I know you have donkeys. Could you take one? Probably not, but I thought I'd take a shot.

"Oh, and also," she added, almost as an afterthought, "we found some border collie puppies on a farm nearby. The owner's been sick and hasn't been on the farm in ages, maybe a couple of years. A nice caretaker feeds the dogs, but they spend most of their lives in a little outbuilding behind a fence and they're alone most of the time. And now the farm is for sale, so they need homes.

"And there's this older border collie—about three, I think—who's the father. Quite a character. He's not housebroken. I don't think he's ever lived in a house or been around people much, just the caretaker. He's been fed and cared for, but never trained or given any kind of work. Flo's seen the dogs; she knows them. Call me if you can help."

I saw her agenda right away: She was calling about that older dog. Having pitched the retired donkeys many times before, she knew I wouldn't take them. And finding homes for adorable puppies is rarely a problem.

In fact, I made a few calls about the puppies, and placed two of them in minutes, giving the interested parties Amy's phone number. I didn't want to call her back myself; that was the safest course.

But the story of the older dog stuck in my head. I could envision a border collie behind a fence all day, probably wearing a groove in the dirt as he ran along the fence day and night.

I was a bit chewed up at the time, still dealing with the loss of my soulmate Orson. I'd had to put him down after he bit several people. His death was a recent wound and a big one, perhaps one that would never completely heal.

Yet the abandoned animal has always particularly touched me, even more than an abused one, oddly. Carol the Lonely Donkey was an example. Even Pearl, though hardly abused or neglected, had been in a crate at the veterinary clinic for many weeks while she recovered from surgery, a distressing isolation for so sociable a dog. I was eager to take her in, and she was happy to come.

A bit curious, and a bit apprehensive, I called Amy's friend Flo, who knew these dogs. She and Amy had teamed up to get the border collies into good homes before the farm was sold. It was a nice thing to do.

The older dog's name was Izzy, Flo said. He was a New Zealand–bred black-and-white, and he was "gorgeous."

He had spent several years in a small house built for dogs. It had no heat, so on particularly bitter nights, the caretaker took him into his trailer, but not often, since Izzy had never been housebroken. Otherwise, he lived in his little compound with an older, spayed female.

He and the caretaker's dog, a female border collie, did, in fact, run along the fences, the female on the outside, Izzy on the inside, wearing a deep trail. Then a few months ago, Izzy somehow escaped the fence, which was why there were now puppies.

"He's such a beautiful dog, but he's never been with people," said Flo, a friend of the caretaker. "Hard to place, because he's kind of wild, not trained, and not neutered. But he's a loving dog," she added quickly. "Very alert. Very tuned in to people when he sees them."

The farm owners, one a writer from the city, had bought the place a few years earlier and undertaken extensive renovations. They bought the border collies with the idea that they'd also acquire sheep. But they hadn't; in fact, they seemed to have given up on the idea of the farm altogether and hardly even showed up there.

Izzy was tended to by the caretaker. "He filled the food bowl," Flo reported, "and made sure the dogs had water. He didn't have time for much else."

I drove the half hour to the farm the next morning. It was a beautiful spread, with a carefully restored old farmhouse, a barn-turned-writer's-studio that I coveted, and acres of hills and meadows, gardens and ponds.

On the hill near where Flo and I had parked, I saw a black-

and-white dog racing along the fence line, opposite a brown-and-white border collie running along outside.

"Izzy!" yelled Flo, but he barely responded. It occurred to me he might not know his name.

As we got closer, I could see that Flo was right: With his golden eyes and elegant—though badly matted—coat, he was a remarkably handsome dog, full of instinct and personality. He also seemed, like many working dogs that chase in circles all day, a bit mad.

Orson had been the same way when he came to me, which gave me pause. I loved Orson dearly, and he had done much for me, but his life had ended sorrowfully and too soon. I didn't want to experience anything like that again. Still, I had learned so much. Maybe I could get it right this time. That thought had drawn me since I'd first heard Amy's message.

Flo and I opened the gate and entered the compound. The older female scurried nervously into the dog house; a woman in Vermont had already agreed to take her in. Izzy raced over, ignored me, and jumped up on Flo. He was almost frantic, his tongue long on this warm Saturday.

He retreated long enough to give me a quick sniff and a bark, then rushed back to jump at Flo again, then dashed back along the fence. He dropped to the ground, spun around, so overjoyed to have some attention that he was hardly in control of himself.

I called him to me and offered him a treat; he didn't even notice it. But he lay down and showed me his belly, and I crouched down for a better look. His teeth seemed fine; his weight was perfect, his muscles firm. Except for the dirty, matted fur, he was in great condition, and eager for affection. But he'd need months, perhaps years, of training to calm down, and more appropriate work than running fences.

I wasn't sure he was for me. In such a state, he was too crazed to be a Bedlam Farm dog; he would drive me nuts. But I was sure that with a little training he'd be easy to place elsewhere.

I guess I'd kind of known this would happen.

HE'D NEVER BEEN IN A CAR BEFORE, SO I HAD TO LIFT IZZY INTO THE back of my Blazer, where he scuttled from side to side, his tongue growing longer.

Back home, I opened the rear door and slipped a collar and leash on him and he hopped out, wild-eyed. In the yard, Pearl, Clem, and Rose all came up to the gate, sniffing and wagging, unthreatening—but Izzy curled his lip. I sat down on the porch steps and talked to him, and he settled a bit. I gave him some water, which he gulped down.

Then I walked him out back to see the pasture and the don-keys and sheep, which was not a good move. Izzy glanced at the donkeys, froze, slipped out of the collar—and took off in a panic.

While I fruitlessly called his name, he dashed up the road. He had no idea where he was going, just fleeing those large and apparently fearsome donkeys.

I jumped in the Blazer and sped off after him, almost as pan-icked as he was. There were deep woods all around, and if he ca-reened into them, he'd almost surely be lost for good. He had no tags or ID, even if someone found him. And though this was an unpaved country road, people sped along it at reckless speeds.

I caught up with him well up the road, jumped out of the car, and tried to grab him. Izzy did just what I'd feared and veered off into the trees. But then, farther up the road, I saw him pop out of the woods and continue running uphill. At least he was sticking to the road.

I needed Rose. She'd almost always helped me in tight

spots, and this qualified. Izzy didn't know or trust me, was a stranger to the farm and its environs, didn't know his own name, and was in an awful fright. I drove back for my canine first responder. We'd handled many emergencies together.

Still, as we drove toward the small hamlet of Cossayuna, my heart was sinking. Some neighbors were waiting for school buses or collecting their mail; I asked them if they'd seen a dog running by, and they all pointed up the hill.

We were nearly two miles from the farm when I saw Izzy far up ahead, galloping along Bunker Hill Road. He was probably doing twenty miles an hour. I gunned the Blazer and roared past him. I yelled his name but he was still frenzied, running flat out. The donkeys, gentle as they were, had scared him senseless.

I pulled up a quarter mile ahead, to an abandoned red-brick schoolhouse that stands alone at the intersection of two country lanes. In a few minutes I saw a black-and-white blur—astonishingly, still running—coming toward me. I opened the car door and yelled to Rose, who bounded out, looking around in some confusion about her mission. I pointed to the approaching Izzy.

This was another of those many situations for which there are no real commands, but Rose was a master at grasping the task at hand. I yelled, "Get that dog! Get that dog!" and as he came racing past, she tore off after him, grabbing on to the fur of his tail. He was startled and spun around, which broke the trance.

Rose looked to me for further instructions, but I didn't have any. She gave him a warning growl, then came back to me. I dropped to my knees and held out my arms to the escapee. He was spent, sides heaving, his tongue dragging almost to the road. "Izzy," I said softly. "It's okay. Come here."

His fever had passed, it seemed, and he looked at me, then at Rose. He walked over and dropped to the ground. I patted his head and rubbed his belly, which seemed to calm him. Then I picked him up—he felt nearly limp with exhaustion—and put him in the car. Rose hopped in with him. No hard feelings, they lay down beside each other as we drove back to the farm.

Back in the fenced yard, he drank some water, then began obsessively peeing on every bush, tree, and post. I remembered that he wasn't neutered and reminded myself to remedy that. I went into the house for more water and when I came out, Izzy had jumped the fence and was peering around the corner of the house, at the donkeys.

WE HAD PLENTY OF TROUBLE THAT FIRST WEEK. IZZY DESTROYED two crates while I was out, damaging walls and floors in the process. Yet I had no choice but to crate him. He was unhousebroken and completely unfamiliar with houses; sounds like a running dishwasher panicked him. He freaked out at the very idea of taking a walk, something he'd never done. When I gave him a bone, he initially had no idea what to do with it.

But he seemed to want to work with me. I started his training by giving him liver treats—a big hit—and saying his name over and over. Then I taught him the useful phrases "sit," "lie down," and "stay."

I fed him in his crate and kept it near me in my office, so that he not only got used to it, but began seeing it as a retreat and safe haven from his confusing new world.

An astonishingly bright dog, he had good role models in Rose and the other dogs, and quickly picked up the idea of walking in the woods with us, although he still circled frantically. And he figured out how to respond to a marrow bone. Chewing bones is calming for dogs, gives them something to do, and satisfies several basic instincts.

I also took him to my vet to have him neutered, confident it would help calm him and ease some of his obsessive "marking" outdoors and in.

Our first few days reminded me of how far I had come. For me, training is about bonding and patience more than a particular technique. If you've made a connection with a dog, if you can keep your mouth shut and stay with it, wonderful things can happen.

First, Izzy learned his name, so he paid attention to me, always the first step. Commands like "sit" and "lie down" were grounding, calming. He was a dog that loved to work with people, and day by day he became less frantic.

Happily, he and the other dogs accepted one another without aggression, posturing, or jockeying for position. Pearl isn't physically dominant, but as a champion show dog, she'd developed bearing and authority. Few dogs challenge her, nor does she deign to quarrel with them. Clem simply loves every living thing. And Rose seemed to appreciate having another border collie to run with. I noticed her and Izzy often sitting together in the yard. The Labs and the border collies had paired up, as members of the same breed often do.

Izzy, who, like Pearl, appeared to be a dog waiting for the right human to come along, seemed to relish becoming part of the tribe. Each morning, he licked the other dogs when he emerged from his crate. He still slept in the crate, something I would continue for months, until he'd completely settled in. This was his place to feel safe, and it gave me time off and ease of mind, too.

When I read or watched TV, he plopped down at my feet and didn't move. During my writing hours, he crawled under the desk—as Orson used to—and lay absolutely still.

Eating was no problem. I put a small chunk of hamburger

in the microwave each morning, and dropped some warm burger and juice into each bowl of dry kibble, to ensure that all four dogs would eat promptly, polishing off their own breakfasts, not one another's.

At first, Izzy inched toward Rose's bowl or Clementine's—he didn't dare make a move at Pearl's—but once he realized that he'd get plenty, he backed off.

It was a welcome sign of amiability for four dogs to eat side by side.

Twice a day, on a short leash, I took him out to see the once fearsome donkeys, and he sat or lay down while I offered them cookies or carrots at the pasture gate.

After his initial panic attack, I could see his good breeding show through and help stabilize him. He watched the donkeys carefully but didn't bolt, and after a few days, I could bring him into the pasture and remove his leash without incident. He barely took any notice at all of the sheep.

I told myself that Izzy understood this was home now and he wouldn't run off again. Dogs that are trained, that attach to people and other dogs, that are well fed and cared for, have little reason to go anywhere else, and rarely do.

Of course, we had a way to go toward a placid life together. Since he'd never lived in a house, there were accidents. I shrugged, got the Odor-Off, cleaned up. He would grow out of it, I knew.

I loved him very much, and he had strongly attached himself to me.

After ten days or so, Flo and Amy drove over to see how he was doing. By then, he was sitting, staying, obeying my "no street" command. He would lie down at my side. He liked to tear playfully after Rose, who, after a few skeptical days, seemed to enjoy having him around.

"Wow," Amy said, beaming. "Izzy hit the jackpot."

"So did I," I said.

YET IF ANYBODY OUGHT TO KNOW THE PARTICULAR CHALLENGES and foibles of border collies, it should be me.

I've lived, worked, and matched wits with them for years. Some, like Orson, have been as troublesome and difficult as they are loving. Then there's Rose, thoroughly sensible and professional.

Either way, I should know better than to relax too soon. I was foolish to buy into Izzy's initial routine. After recovering from his neutering, and adapting with quiet caution to his new environs, his demonic, intelligent, ferociously independent self emerged.

We began the game of border collie chess. The first real trouble arose when he kept showing up outside the fenced yard. First move (his): He tunneled under a gate. My move: I rolled a boulder against the gate, blocking his exit. But Izzy used the boulder as a launching pad that made it simple to leap over the gate. I countered by leaning rakes and shovels outside the gate to block the airspace. He countercountered by plowing right through them.

Anthony, working on the barn one morning, looked up to see Izzy lifting a chain latch with his teeth. I put an additional hook on the fencepost.

Since Izzy still wasn't thoroughly housebroken and remained prone to marking, I crated him when I went out. His move: I came home one night from dinner and was shocked to see that he'd demolished his crate. He'd nosed open the latch (or perhaps I'd closed it improperly) and had somehow pushed aside the plastic tray on the bottom of the crate; it was bent and broken. Then, perhaps out of anxiety, he'd had diarrhea all over the crate and the floor.

My move: I drove forty-five minutes to Saratoga to get a tougher crate. The next night while I was away, he flipped it over and pushed through a corner; his thrashing chipped paint off the walls and tore a rug. Yet when I was at home, he spent entire nights in the crate with complete equanimity.

His actions were hard to reconcile. He had little of Orson's ferocious territoriality. He loved to cuddle with people, to have strangers scratch his belly. He'd happily lie by my side for hours. But he had to be with me.

This separation stuff is often a big issue for people with dogs. A dog loves you so much that he simply can't stand it when you leave—a lot of us like to see it that way. The devoted dog is so faithful to its master that life without him is unbearable.

I grasped the dramatic potential of the Izzy-and-Katz saga: Lonely dog living in isolation for years attaches to border collie–loving man with sheep who has just lost his beloved canine companion.

The truth was likely more nuanced: Unsocialized rescue dog feels unsafe—even panic-stricken—when he cannot locate the human who now feeds him. My other dogs, who arrived as puppies, are untroubled by my comings and goings; they know I will be back. They love me, but none of them chews things, gets into garbage, or freaks out in his crate when I go out to dinner.

So why does Izzy?

Because re-homed dogs are apt to be more anxious, to have more behavioral problems, to require long, patient training. Because border collies, bristling with instinct and drive, are prone to behavioral problems when traumatized. Izzy was not an abused dog, but neither was he grounded, trained, or socialized.

My guess was that he grew terrified when I left him alone. To attribute his panicky behavior to great love was tempting, but probably wouldn't help the dog. I needed to acclimate him to my departures and returns, to train him, which, in turn, would soothe him.

I called for an appointment with a veterinary acupuncturist in Vermont. Her massage and acupuncture and the Chinese herbs she'd prescribed had helped calm Orson, and Izzy was, most of the time, a less frantic dog. Here we went again.

I also took him to my regular vet for blood work and stool samples, to make sure there wasn't some physical or biological trigger prompting these meltdowns.

And I steeled myself. To be patient. To be creative. To be realistic. I had been here before.

In some ways, training and retraining Orson, I had succeeded: He had learned a great deal, had adapted to my household and routines, loved and was loved by many. Yet, in the most fundamental way, I'd failed; I'd lost him.

So I knew that taking on Izzy was a real commitment, a substantial one. It wouldn't proceed in a straight line, a simple matter of classes over hours or weeks. It could take years of training, conditioning, and reinforcing, meanwhile cleaning up accidents and damage, tolerating setbacks and applauding progress.

With Izzy, a dog I now very much wanted to keep, I was in for a long haul. With Orson, I could tell myself I didn't know what I was in for. This time, I did.

Izzy was a complex animal, probably the most intelligent dog I'd ever had. He watched, absorbed, remembered.

The curious thing was that he eagerly went into the crate, and often spent quiet hours resting inside. I wasn't sure precisely what triggered his frenzied escape efforts, but I had the gnawing sensation it was his attachment to me. He'd been waiting for a human for a long time, and now that he'd found one, he meant to hang on.

My move. I went online, did some homework, and located a traveling crate approved for airline use. Its latches were all outside his reach; the interiors were all smooth plastic. It seemed to hold him, at least for now.

THE FOLLOWING WEEK, I WAS VISITING THE DONKEYS, FEEDING JEANnette a cookie, scratching baby Jesus, when a black streak came rocketing up the pasture. Izzy. He'd escaped the front yard, where he'd been sitting companionably with Rose, then crawled under the pasture gate. I could see Rose watching, nonplussed, as he made his way toward me.

The donkeys weren't nervous around Izzy, and he never bothered them. The sheep, less trusting, moved uneasily to the farthest corner of the pasture. Reflexively and typically, I started screaming at Izzy to lie down, but then I caught myself. Let's see what happens, I thought. Give him a chance.

Izzy looked at me, then up at the sheep as if noticing them for the first time. He dropped into the border collie crouch, and started giving the sheep a lot of eye. Good working dogs control sheep with their stares, not their teeth.

The sheep picked up on this, huddled together, and froze. Izzy crept slowly up toward the sheep. I kept still.

Without any commands from me, he moved slowly to the left of the herd, then behind it. Border collies who know what they're doing, who are properly trained, don't run straight toward sheep. They do what's called an "outrun," moving around and behind the flock so that the sheep move away from the dog, toward the herder. By using voice commands—"come bye," "away"—you can instruct the dog to move the sheep to the right or left, closer or farther away. Border collies have speed and enormous stamina; they can, if necessary, race around in front of the sheep to stop them. The flock can be controlled that way, moved where the herder wants them to go.

Izzy, I was surprised to see, was cool as dry ice as he moved closer. Plenty of border collies go nuts in that situation, too aroused to control themselves, let alone the sheep. But Izzy was going slow. The sheep were nervous but not panicked, a good sign.

As he curved behind them, they started trotting down the hill, and he seemed startled. It was always at this point that Orson lost it; once the sheep moved, he couldn't help chasing them, and herding became hunting. The sheep, sensing this, ran for their lives. With Izzy, still using a lot of eye, they started to run, then stopped.

Izzy looked at me, but I had no appropriate commands to offer; because we'd done no training, he wouldn't understand. I just pointed to the right of the flock and said, "Izzy, there." He paused, then ran to where I was pointing. The sheep slowed and began walking toward me, Izzy behind them. I hustled over to open the gate of the training pen, and the sheep filed inside.

"Pen!" I shouted joyously. "This is the pen!" I called Izzy and he came right to me and lay down next to the pen.

This was a staggering accomplishment, especially for a first attempt. Izzy had a lot of instinct, but not aggression. He wanted to work; I had work for him to do. It was tough to believe he'd never herded sheep before.

Thrilled, I decided we'd begin regular herding training the next morning, and continue every day thereafter. A working dog who could effectively push sheep around wouldn't need to destroy crates or chase trucks, I hoped. He'd have better, more important things to do. He could match wits with the sheep instead of with me. And then, he could stay.

Elvis learns to stay.

"Jon, Do You Have a Cow?"

ALICE AND HARVEY HAHN COME BY ONCE A WEEK TO HELP CLEAN up the farmhouse. I would hate to live here without their help in mopping and swabbing away the crud and dust that invariably gets tracked back in within hours, not to mention the universal coating of dog hair.

It's become a sort of ritual for Alice and Harvey to enter the house, toting various brooms and brushes, and ask me a quiet, earnest question: "Jon, is that a new dog?" Or "Jon, is there a baby donkey in the pasture?" Or "Jon, was that a cat we saw out by the barn?"

Today's question from Alice: "Jon, do you have a cow?"

Nothing they saw hereabouts seemed to surprise them any longer, so when I said yes, I had acquired a cow, she simply nodded and said what they always say: "Why, we never quite know what to expect. You are becoming a real farmer now, I guess." And then they went to work.

I did have a cow. In fact, I'd had to punch my new Brown Swiss steer Elvis in the nose that very morning, not something I was proud of. But it was really more of a tap on the nose, and he had it coming.

Elvis weighs eighteen hundred pounds and is roughly the size of a mobile home. He'd snuck up behind me, grabbed the hood of my sweatshirt with his mouth. That I was wearing the sweatshirt seemed of no concern to him. I felt my feet lift off the ground; he was dangling me the way a Lab enjoys a smelly sock.

So I wriggled around and slugged him in the nose. He put me down, but seemed startled, even hurt, and I felt bad. I wondered if a cow could be trained.

Elvis could use training. "We've never seen quite so friendly a cow," my farmer friends kept telling me, and it was true. When people enter the pasture, Elvis comes running. The effect is rather like a two-story building lifting off its foundations and charging down a hill. You just pray it can stop if it wants to. And that it will want to.

Elvis slurps faces and hands with his enormous tongue. He grabs at shirts and hats, nuzzles butts. If you sit on the ground, he'll put his head in your lap, providing he doesn't sit on top of you—his landings are neither graceful nor accurate.

Getting Elvis to stop or stay wasn't about his learning etiquette or performing tricks. He meant only affection, but if he had trouble slowing, the human in his path could end up mush.

One incentive I could use in this mission was apples. I'd been on my way to give the donkeys a few that morning when Elvis spotted them and came lumbering over.

He snatched one apple out of my hand, inhaled it, let out an enthusiastic bellow, and began nosing my pockets for others.

After that, when I reached the pasture gate, held up an apple, and yelled, "Elvis, come," he trotted right over. If he got too intimate or pushy—bumping me, drooling on me, sticking his head too close—I flicked him on the nose with two fingers and he backed right up. Then I held up one hand and loudly said, "Stay!" in the enthusiastic voice dog trainers always recommend. To my amazement, and the shock of my neighbors, he stayed.

People in town began showing up to see my sort-of-trained cow. Cows are widely supposed, in these environs, to be stupid. "I'm not sure if it's an unusual thing, or if nobody ever tried to do it before," observed my friend Peter Hanks, a dairy farmer and photographer. "But he is an unusual cow."

Peter should know. Elvis had been his cow.

PETER HAS BEEN FARMING FOR FORTY YEARS AND IS DECIDEDLY UN-sentimental, to say the least, about livestock. He's been milking cows or sending them to market most of his life. They're his livelihood; he literally cannot afford to become emotionally attached to them.

Cows like Elvis are usually treated well—they're investments, after all—but hardly catered to. They're rarely outside anymore; land prices make it hard to raise cows on pasture. So they live in dairy barns and are fed silage, a sour-smelling mixture of ground-up corn and hay. They're not expected to have stimulating lives, laced with affection. The males, and the females once past their prime breeding and milking years, are sent to market.

So I was a bit surprised when Peter showed up at my farm one day, mumbling about a steer he'd named Brownie.

He'd never seen a cow quite like this one, Peter said. Brownie followed him around. He licked him. "He didn't want to get on the market truck, so he hung around me like a dog," Peter reported. "He seemed to have figured things out."

For the first time, he confessed, he simply could not bear to send a cow to market (translation: the slaughterhouse). He was surprised, and a bit embarrassed.

Farmers live by simple, hard codes: You don't waste a bullet on a chicken. (If it is injured or sick, you dispatch it with an ax.) You don't spend more on vet bills than an animal will fetch at market. And you don't keep a cow as a pet.

Wow, that must be some cow, I thought, wondering why Peter was telling me this story. Then I realized that he'd come to the one person he knew who was stupid or crazy enough to take in a monster like that.

Peter was between a rock and a hard place. There was no way he could keep a steer off the market truck for long; he'd be jeered at all over town. Merely to have given the animal a name was suspect. But to give Brownie away would bring even greater shame. Farmers don't keep animals because they are sweet, and they don't turn them into eighteen-hundred-pound gifts.

"Am I guessing right?" I asked incredulously. "You want me to take this cow, which I will have to buy tons of hay for every year—and *pay* you for the privilege?" I was already imagining trying to explain this to Paula, still adjusting to the expense of four donkeys.

But the truth was, I'd been yearning for a cow for some time. Perhaps not as intelligent or affectionate as donkeys, there nonetheless seems something soulful and philosophical about them. I like the way they stare meaningfully at nothing with great concentration. They seemed to understand patience and equanimity, traits I was still trying to acquire. They appeared peaceful, accepting of their fate. Or perhaps, as rumored, too dumb to object.

Peter and I commenced weeks of the obligatory haggling that goes into any major purchase involving a farm. Haggling is expected, and I'd learned that farmers can take offense if you don't join in.

When I first bought hay, Danny Thomas explained that his $3.75-per-bale price was worth every cent. "It's good, nutritious, second cut," he harrumphed. Fine, I said, taking out the checkbook.

"It's heavy and well baled," Danny insisted.

"Good," I said.

"Perfect for sheep, even though I know you won't like the price."

Finally I got the message and began grumping about the texture, consistency, and price. I poked the bale with my finger. I chewed on a handful (I knew tasting was expected, as with good wines, though it would be months before I learned what hay was supposed to feel or taste like).

Finally, after much back-and-forth, we agreed on $3.75, the price Danny had asked in the first place. He seemed happier.

So Peter and I started weeks of haggling—in person, on the phone, via e-mail.

The cow could bring eighty cents a pound at market, Pete argued, and given his size, that was a lot of money. He brought over printouts of USDA and commodity-market prices to make his point.

But we weren't sending him to market, I pointed out.

I might get tired of Brownie, Pete said, especially of feeding him. I might send him to market. Clearly he wasn't about to court ridicule by donating a giant steer that I could turn around and sell at a profit a few weeks later.

If I did sell the cow, I had to split the proceeds with him, Pete argued. Fine, I said, for the first two years. After that, any revenue should be mine to keep.

We settled on $500, a bargain price (although there were some, including my wife, who couldn't see the logic in paying for a cow that performed no useful function, consumed two or three bales of hay a day in winter, and almost surely never would be sent to market).

Before we shook on the deal, Annie, my farm helper, and I went to visit Brownie in Pete's barns. Rose came along. Pete was telling the truth: All the other cows kept eating or backed away when we approached, but one came right to the gate, licked Annie's arm, and put his massive head on my shoulder. He also leaned down to sniff Rose, who matter-of-factly nipped his nose. "I'm not your friend" was the message, which was also the truth.

The barn was typical of modern dairy farms, but it wasn't a bright or cheerful place. Annie, who wants good lives for all creatures, urged that we take the steer. "He would be so happy on the farm. He could be outside, have pasture, neat things to look at," she said. "And he wouldn't go to slaughter."

Offering a cow visual stimulation was not among my key goals, but Brownie did seem a gentle soul. In the fenced paddock behind my big barn, he could graze, gaze, walk around a bit. An artesian well—a great bonus on a working farm—supplied water all year.

The big issue was hay. I'd have to buy many more bales for next winter.

Notions of usefulness vary, I told my wife. This was an unusual creature. He would fit in. I decided to name him Elvis, as he seemed a good ole boy.

Peter and I reached an accord, including purchase price and many complex profit-sharing options should things change down the road. It was the first time in his farming career that he'd kept a cow from slaughter. Although he wouldn't admit it, I could tell he was pleased with the deal.

ON A SUNNY SPRING DAY, PETER BACKED HIS LIVESTOCK TRAILER UP to my back paddock and opened the door. After some thumping around, a brown behemoth came lumbering out, looking disoriented and anxious.

Five or six of us were standing around, awaiting his arrival, and we all said the same thing at precisely the same time: "Oh my God."

Seen alone, without the rest of his herd, Elvis was enormous. Staggering. The ground shook when he moved.

He seemed mesmerized by everything he saw. He sniffed, stared, and drooled, wide-eyed and restless. I wondered if he was looking for other cows.

Annie brought Elvis some fistfuls of hay—something he'd never eaten before—and he grabbed a mouthful, which seemed to settle him down quite a bit. He allowed Annie and then me to stroke his neck.

Pete watched the proceedings for a few minutes, then got back into his truck and drove off. "Good luck, Elvis," he shouted. "You're a lucky cow." Elvis turned and watched him drive away.

At first, Elvis seemed nervous about being alone. Next day, he saw Paula in the adjacent pasture brushing the donkeys and simply walked through the fence and trotted over to visit her.

Visions of broken bones (hers, if Elvis trotted over her feet) or other severe injuries (his, if he went through a second fence and out onto the road) sent her inside, promptly. "He's bigger than our first house," she said, calling me on the cell phone; I was at a neighbor's. "I don't want to snuggle with him."

I rushed home and found Elvis alone, staring forlornly at the sheep huddled way up at the top of the pasture. Perhaps the hill was too steep for him to climb. Perhaps he was awaiting an invitation.

I'd never owned a cow before, or tried to get one to do something it didn't want to. I could only hope that Elvis had no idea how big he was.

"Elvis, let's go home," I said, and I began walking back to the paddock. Possibly abashed, he trotted after me.

Anthony rushed over to put up a single-strand electrified wire around the paddock. Elvis got buzzed once, then never approached the fence again.

Maybe he no longer wanted to. Everybody who saw the steer in the following days agreed that he seemed quite content to munch hay, take in the sun, and stare out at the view. Annie socialized him relentlessly, bringing him hay, brushing him, stroking his neck.

"I never saw such a cow," said one local, who'd grown up on a dairy farm. "Are you sure he isn't a big dog?"

ARE COWS REALLY AS DUMB AND SINGLE-MINDED ABOUT EATING AS people say? Hard to know. They haven't been allowed to be smart like dogs. We don't take them for walks, throw balls for them, give them work or changes of scenery. Long domesticated, they haven't lived in the wild since medieval times. We tend to think of them as walking chunks of meat, or milk machines, if we think of them at all.

But Elvis has changed my attitude about cows. He may not be a scholar, but he is very social. He loves Annie. He loves people. When I take the dogs out for their morning walk, he bellows repeatedly until I bring him an apple. Anthony, no sentimentalist when it comes to animals, had to concede that Elvis is "a pretty neat cow."

He seems delighted to be outside. He rolls huge round bales of hay into position and snuggles next to them. (When he lies down, you can feel the vibrations all the way to the farmhouse.) He appreciates the view over the valley and gazes out at other farms with other cows much of the day.

Plus, I cannot begin to say how proud I am of our training. Elvis doesn't much grab clothes or shirts anymore, comes when called, stays when asked. Not all my dogs will do those things as reliably.

Once or twice a week, he has a bout of bovine madness and goes dancing around the pasture in little playful bursts, prancing in circles, trying to entice the donkeys to join in. Trees shake.

It's fun to watch cars coming down the road screech to a stop when they see this apparition looming before them.

I'm very pleased to have him join the team, even though it will cost me a bundle to feed him.

"I wonder if you could get him to sit or lie down," a neighbor asked me in all seriousness. I guess we'll find out.

Ben, Mo, and Anthony

FIVE

Grunt and Grumble

ANTHONY AND HIS WIFE, HOLLY, WERE HAVING SUNDAY breakfast with me at Bea's on Main Street when he ran into a contractor buddy named Danny. This was a signal: Let the Grunt and Grumble begin.

Anthony is one of the best Grunt and Grumblers I've met. He stood up and commenced a ferocious round.

He and Danny complained about the cost of tractors and lumber, debated quality concrete and insulation, bemoaned the cost of fuel. The conversation went on awhile, but neither man seemed to give a thought to the families left sitting behind with their pancakes, nor did the families appear to mind.

Anthony and Danny had considerable respect for one another. I had the sense they were feeling each other out a bit, perhaps with an eye toward working together, though I understood virtually nothing of what they were saying.

It went approximately like this:

Danny: "So did you talk to Ted Hughes?"

Anthony: "Yeah, I talked to him."

Danny: "So what are you guys going to do?"

Anthony: "We're going to dig out behind the garage and get all the shale out, and then I'm going to get the five-yard minimum of concrete—"

Danny: "Right."

Anthony: "—and pour a regular pad there, Alaskan-slab style."

Pause.

Danny: "How're you gonna frame it?"

Anthony: "Just regular two-by-four construction. Side it with T-111 to match what's there."

Danny: "Uh-huh, good." Both men had folded their arms by now, their leg stances widening.

Danny: "And what about that rotted-out sill?"

Anthony: "We're gonna cut in a door to the old wall with a header and two posts. Then just knock out the sill and replace it with two three-by-six pressure-treated."

People in the crowded restaurant just stepped around them, unbothered, but after ten minutes, both men raised both hands at the same time, either a spontaneous gesture or some sort of accepted secret Grunt and Grumble signal. Enough. Back to breakfast.

"I tell my wife, 'Don't even talk to me on the days when I have to gas up the trucks,'" Danny said, a parting sally. And that was that, at least for this round.

But the next round wouldn't be far off. I've heard Anthony and his pals Grunt and Grumble about demanding clients, the best way to polyurethane pine, truck suspensions, and the merits of buying supplies at the local hardware store as opposed to Lowe's or Home Depot.

Grunt and Grumble is conducted pretty much like a David Mamet play—sentences go unfinished, assumptions are made, key words savored, in a kind of rhythmic incantation. Everyone who does good Grunt and Grumble understands everything the other Grumblers are saying, or pretends to.

Nothing is ever questioned or explained, unless somebody like me is there, saying, "Huh?" and "What?" I don't do that anymore. I just nod and mumble the occasional "Yup," which buys some time.

Grunt and Grumble is not limited to contractors and builders. Farmers are among the best Grunt and Grumble slingers on the planet. "Jeez, we need rain! Else my corn will fall over of its own weight and die." Weather always works. From there, they usually segue into tractors and mowers, market prices, the outrageous cost and behavior of vets. Town road crews and volunteer firefighters have their own variants.

A Grunt and Grumble session can erupt at any time or place. There's an associated physical position: It works best if your arms are folded. If you are thin and young, like Anthony, you fold your arms and lean back. Most Grunt and Grumblers lean forward and rest their folded arms on their substantial bellies. Either way, you take a wide stance, spread your legs two or three feet apart, settle in. This way guys battered by hard physical labor can Grunt and Grumble for many minutes, while easing back pain and shifting the pressure from one sore foot to the other.

Veteran Grunt and Grumblers also lean on their trucks or tractors, as the smell of testosterone and diesel fuel mix in about equal proportions.

Anthony and I used to squabble about the time spent on this mumbling, until he convinced me that Grunt and Grumbling is not a waste of time, not mere bullshitting or goofing off. It's essential to functioning in rural life, part gossip and news, part education, even part (*shhh*) support group. Friendships are made, deals struck, information gleaned about everything from which trailer tows what ATV to where deer have been tracked.

Farmer A learns what his neighbor Farmer C is doing about his cows from Farmer B. Gossip is idle chatter; Grunt and Grumbling is business.

And, also, part philosophy. Most men upstate do not have deep emotional discussions about their lives and anxieties. Yet they have real fears—rising taxes and the brutal toll of high gas prices, the difficulties of finding skilled workers in a region where the young tend to flee. The quixotic, unrealistic expectations of clients and consumers. The relentless problems with backs and legs and knees. The unpredictable tacks and turns of the marketplace (after Hurricane Katrina, for example, the price of lumber shot way up, increasing the cost of construction even this far away, making everyone unhappy). All of that emerges, sometimes in code, in these conversations.

By and large, there is little leering or chatter about women. It's a time for busy men to talk about work.

Grunt and Grumbling—I've been timing it—usually lasts ten to fifteen minutes, the end signaled by one guy either looking at his watch and seeming shocked at the time ("Oh, jeez, the wife will think I'm dead") or an abrupt "Well, yup." Sometimes there's a concluding lament: "That well ain't gonna get dug in here, is it?" or "Guess I ain't gonna make any money standing here."

Grunt and Grumble can erupt spontaneously at construction sites where other Grunt and Grumblers stop by to inspect and to chat. But you can also reliably find it at places like Stewart's, a local convenience store/gas station chain, at the post office, at the hardware store, or any place that sells tools.

Once I grasped this, certain behaviors made more sense to me. I'd puzzled for months, for example, about why Anthony drove to Stewart's for his morning juice and bagel when his wife, Holly, offered the same breakfast menu at home. Then, joining him one morning, I understood the ritual.

He heads for Stewart's about seven a.m. His ride-along dog, a genial black Lab, waits in the truck cab. Mo goes everywhere with Anthony and can plop down in the middle of a construction site next to a roaring, belching earthmover and sleep for hours. He also seems to grasp Grunt and Grumbling and waits it out with patience, while I squirm restlessly.

In Stewart's, waiting for his bagel to toast, Anthony launched into some abbreviated Grunt and Grumble with the other men picking up coffee and eggwiches. "Hey, you hear they shut down work on the Marquette place because there's no permit?" This led to intense grumbling about the county building inspectors.

Also, Jamie got a hundred-and-forty-dollar ticket for speeding and for having no lights or license on the trailer that hauls his tractor. This generated an exchange of data on current speed traps. Further, there were reports that somebody in Dorset wanted to sell a few tons of gravel.

A stream of other Grunt and Grumblers came in and out. Early-morning Grunt and Grumbling stays fairly brief—everybody needs to get going, get to work. The farmers were simultaneously generating their own Grunt and Grumble at the Agway or other farm supply stores and tractor dealers.

Anthony collected his bagel and juice and left, exchanging

brief macho banter (just poking and kidding on the fly, very different from true Grunt and Grumbling) with two or three guys.

Back in the truck, Anthony ate only half his bagel. The rest, though he claimed he'd eat it later, was really for Mo, who waited innocently until Anthony was out of the cab, then scarfed the other half down.

Further grumbling comes later on, interspersed during a long and tiring day. From my observations, though, Grunt and Grumbling ceases around four p.m. The men are tired, and it's time to clean up, get home, eat dinner, play with the kids, and rest.

I'm learning some decent Grunt and Grumble myself. I have the stance and the wardrobe—rumpled, dusty clothes, shoes that smell of manure—plus the big belly, bad back, and flat feet. I have the subject matter: hay, sheep, and dogs, and now a cow. I more or less have the attitude, too: The world is a tough and unpredictable place; work is hard; politicians are buttheads; many people are jerks; and, oh well, life goes on.

Yet I'm still developing my style. In the more populous places I lived before, people get nervous when large, strange men approach to chat. Business is mostly private, kept to oneself. Networking occurs at dinner parties and lunches, or around office coolers.

So, in addition to knowing little about insulation or framing, I'm still green at the whole thing. I may never hold my own with the pros. But I'll keep at it.

At least I've developed an appreciation of the form. One April morning, stopping at Stewart's to get the New York papers for Paula and some coffee for myself, I could only listen in speechless admiration as two guys in front of me poured enormous quantities of cream and sugar into their cardboard coffee cups.

    Man in blue cap: "Hey."

    Man in red cap: "Hey."

    Blue Cap: "So, you still working over at—"

    Red Cap: "Yup."

    Blue: "You get your—"

    Red: "Yeah, all fixed."

    Blue: "I bet it was—"

    Red: "More than two grand. . . ."

    Blue: "Ouch. So you lost—"

    Red: "'Bout a week. I'll be done Friday."

    Then they paid for their coffee, waved to each other, and drove off.

Rose at work

_____

SIX

The Loneliness of Rose

SOMETIMES, THE MEASURE OF HOW MUCH WE LOVE AND NEED AN AN-
imal can only be taken when he or she is out of the picture. I'd
constantly bragged about Rose and how important she was to
life on the farm, but it had been a somewhat intellectual appreciation.

And then, one day in early spring, she was not there.

Rose had been sick for a couple of days, vomiting a lot, pausing only long enough to herd sheep. I waited too long to take her
to the vet because that seemed unremarkable: One of my dogs is
often throwing up, especially in spring and summer. I cut back
on food, provide plenty of water and vet-approved antacids, and
the digestive problem usually disappears in a day or two.

This gastrointestinal stuff is part of the downside of my
dogs' freedom and stimulation on the farm. They run into po-

tential dangers and don't always know what's good for them. They can encounter rabid raccoons or skunks, loops of rusted old barbwire in the woods, fleas and ticks and rotting carcasses.

Rose, in particular, lives to work; torn paw pads, Lyme disease, and a host of other afflictions have rarely deterred or even slowed her.

But her vomiting blood was something new. I called the vet at once. He took X-rays.

She'd eaten something with bones, he reported, shards of which had lodged in her stomach and colon. He'd need to keep and watch her for a couple of days before deciding whether the material would pass normally or whether Rose would need surgery. It was a serious condition, he said.

I worried about Rose, who'd probably unearthed some skeleton out in the woods. But I worried about myself as well. I'd been away for brief periods, on book tours and visits to New Jersey, but I'd never been on the farm for any length of time without Rose.

It was disorienting. The sheep were far up in the top pasture and I couldn't bring them down if they needed shelter or grain. I wanted Elvis to come into the paddock, but he declined. I had to postpone the vet's annual visit for sheep inoculations. I had to halt rotational grazing—shifting animals to different pastures so that the grass they've grazed down can recover and re-grow—because there was no simple way to move the flock.

I'd been getting up early for herding lessons with Izzy. He had great instincts, it turned out. He circled the sheep, lay down when asked, gave plenty of eye. But he was far from being a working farm dog. He had no understanding yet of the critical directional signals—"come bye" and "away"—that tell the dog how to move the sheep where you want them to go.

With Rose, I could simply say "barn" or "shed" or "pen"—

and point—and she would bring the sheep. We had danced this dance many times in her three years, until even the sheep pretty much knew the drill.

Now her absence was unnerving, reminding me that she was a full partner, my right arm, as essential to being on the farm as hay or water.

I worried that I'd let things go too far, perhaps even weakened her with overwork. Because the big barn was under construction—in danger of toppling over, so Anthony and his crew were jacking it up and tearing it apart—several pasture gates had to be removed, and grazing had grown more complicated.

Rose and I took the sheep over the hill or across the street to the meadow in the morning and evening so that they could have fresh grass, fill their bellies, then be out of the way during the day, when Anthony needed to maneuver with trucks and tools.

To collect them from their hilltop, Rose had to go way up out of sight to find the flock and push them all the way down the hill, across the pasture, through two gates, in and around piles of wood and debris and mounds of displaced rocks and dirt, then across the road and into the meadow. The distances were much too great for me. So I just opened one gate and said, "Bring me the sheep," then put on my iPod and enjoyed the view until they arrived, usually within three or four minutes.

It was hard work for her, though. On the way down, the sheep kept pausing, nervous about all the equipment and disorder, uncertain where to go. Rose had to keep steering them, urging them across the road, to get them where she—and I— wanted them. Then, her tongue hanging nearly to the ground, she sat to await further instructions. When they were done eating, she had to go through the whole operation in reverse.

Now Rose was in no shape for that kind of work and might

not be for some time. And Izzy wasn't ready to step in. So Annie and I had to truck bales of hay to the far pasture and toss them over the fence. There just wasn't enough available grass, this early in spring, for donkeys, sheep, and a steer to eat all day. And considering the barn renovations, the situation might continue for months.

Between chores, I called the vet's office several times a day. Rose was dehydrated, the staff reported, and was on an IV to replenish fluids. She wasn't eating. She was very quiet in her crate. It was a completely unnatural environment, involving everything she hated—idleness, confinement among strange dogs, constant invasive touching and handling.

The second night, after closing, the techs let me come visit her in her crate. She looked miserable, but happy to see me. I opened the crate, and she licked my hand.

A small dog—just thirty-six lean pounds—she was a commanding presence on the farm, rocketing from one field to another, keeping an eye on her charges all the time from out in the field, from the backyard fence, through the windows of the house. People came considerable distances to see her work, took pictures of her, showered her and her proud owner with compliments.

Now I looked at her chart, alarmed at the growing list of medications and procedures: blood and fecal tests, antivomiting and seizure medications, samples for parasites and Lyme, X-rays, catheters, antibiotics. The vet said he was concerned about infection and about damage to the colon.

I left Rose and drove home in the dark, feeling uncertain and a little afraid.

We were lucky this time. The obstructions passed without surgery and, on the fourth day, Rose came home, slimmer and a bit haggard-looking. She still wore a bandage over her IV site,

and I toted bottles of pills for her. We got stern instructions about rest.

Halfway home, my cell phone rang. My friend Peter Hanks was calling to say that several of his new heifers had escaped his barns overnight and were meandering along a busy state highway. He and his neighbor had managed to round up most of the fugitives, but two were still on the run.

He sounded exhausted, even desperate. "It's a riot," he said. "Can Rose help?"

As Pete knew, there wasn't another trained border collie for miles around. Real farmers couldn't afford them and didn't have time to train them. The irony was not lost on me: The people who had working dogs were the ones who didn't really need them. So I was usually delighted when mine could help.

The vet would disapprove. But losing livestock is a serious matter to a farmer, and passing motorists could also get injured. Maybe Rose could conclude the business promptly, without overtiring herself.

I looked over at her; she was poking her head out the window, enjoying the wind in her face. "You want to go to work?" I asked.

I saw her head swivel and her eyes brighten, like a fireman who hears the bell. We drove over.

I pulled into a pasture and let Rosie out. I pointed to two brown heifers dashing around in circles while people ran waving at them, trying to direct them into Pete's trailer.

Rose charged through the fields right at them, circled behind, and they made for the trailer and scrambled aboard. I don't think it took her five minutes.

At home, Rose moved the hungry sheep into the pasture, and then I put her in her crate with some water and watched as she lay down and went to sleep. I can hardly explain how much safer and easier I felt having her back on the farm.

In border collie lore, there comes a moment in herding dogs' lives when they calm down, come into their own.

Rose's moment came last May. I was in the barn with the donkeys. They were badly in need of brushing to help them shed their winter shagginess, and they'd mischievously rearranged all of the lambing gear, as donkeys are wont to do. So I was inside with them, brushing and cleaning up, for about a half hour.

I didn't see Rose, who is usually nearby, watching and waiting, seeking instructions, preparing to launch herself at a task like a missile.

When I came out of the barn and looked up into the pasture, I was surprised to see her small black-and-white figure far up the hill, lying down next to the sheep, which were arrayed in a semicircle behind her, under the shade of the big pine tree.

I'd never seen Rose, who appeared to be asleep, lie down like that right next to the flock—not of her own volition, anyway. She's always vigilant and busy when they're out in the pasture. Even as they graze, she's usually circling, watching, taking notes.

Nor had I ever seen the sheep dozing three feet from her. They will eat near her, but usually stay on their feet.

At first, seeing her up there so still, I was alarmed. Was she okay? Had she collapsed? Then I saw her head rise and she turned to look at me, as peaceful as I could remember seeing her.

Much slower than she when it comes to grasping things sheep-related, I finally recognized what she was telling me.

She was growing up. The sheep were no longer animals to chase and move around; they were becoming her flock, and their care her responsibility. Herding was no longer something she did because she followed my instructions; it had become something she was instinctually beginning to understand.

The beauty of herding sheep with dogs, for me, isn't displaying or winning awards. I'd never entered Rose in any competition. It's the sense of wordless partnership, the moment where the dog's instincts and the herder's experience fuse into something mutually understood. And Rose was approaching that moment, if she wasn't already there. She wasn't merely resting by the tree; she was sitting with her sheep, watching over them, staying among them, comfortable enough with herself and with them to be still.

It was a big moment for her, and for me.

Finally, after two years' grueling work, she felt free and at ease enough to do nothing. This dog had worked so hard for me every single day, at such a fevered pitch, that I'd been wondering if she could ever just enjoy her role in Bedlam. Now, I thought, she could.

I often bumble and stumble, saying the wrong thing at the wrong time, reinforcing the wrong movements, missing something she's seen, talking too much. Rose listens intently, yet she also has the gift of knowing when not to listen. If she saw two ewes drifting away from the herd into the woods and I didn't, she went after them even if I told her to stay. Was that good training? I think so. Over time I had come to respect her judgment.

Now she was also developing an ease and confidence apart from me. "Good for you," I yelled up the hill, for lack of anything better to say, and she cocked her head, wondering what kind of command that was. "Congratulations," I added for good measure.

CERTAIN PEOPLE AND SUBCULTURES IN THE DOG WORLD HAVE ALways irritated or troubled me. People who tell me what their dogs are thinking. People who think the only moral way to acquire a dog is to rescue one that you can claim has been abused.

People who tell me crates are cruel. People who explain that their dogs are obese because they can't bear to say no when the dogs beg at the table. People who tell me that people are always to blame when they get bitten. Trainers who claim a dog can be trained in days. Owners who spend a few thousand bucks on a giant plasma-screen TV but insist, "I'll never pay a lot of money for a dog"—an animal that will live with their family for years.

And last but by no means least, the border collie snobs.

Border collie snobs are invariably well dressed. They travel frequently through Scotland and Ireland and know the names of all the great European herding dogs. The true BCSs favor short-haired border collies because the long-haired ones get their fur caught on burrs and brambles on the moors.

They tend not to favor a variety of approaches to training their dogs but adopt uniform—and very rigid—methods. Those dogs you see winning ribbons on TV don't get there by relaxing and finding their own way. Every move they make— the way they sit, at what distance from the sheep, how they hold their heads—results from intense, almost relentless training. I used to watch in amazement as trainers waited until a dog's head was pointed in precisely the right direction, then click a clicker, over and over again.

This formal training can yield some remarkable results, but it isn't for me. Rose and I have found our own way. That doesn't make us better than anybody else, or even as good, but we probably have a happier time.

Border collies, thanks to cable shows and movies like *Babe,* have seized the public imagination. With their reputed intelligence, their remarkable energy and ability to attach to humans, they touch people.

Frankly, I think their intelligence somewhat debatable. Orson herded school buses and trucks. Rose has thrown herself at a snowplow blade. Not in a million years would Clementine or Pearl pull such a stunt. Are these dogs really bright, or do they just have amazing instincts? Is there a line between smart and nuts?

I'm quite partial to this breed, but I'm wary of glorifying them beyond all proportion.

Rose is a farm dog, without clickers or ribbons. But I wonder how those Discovery Channel dogs would do in the middle of the night in a rainstorm, lambs and ewes and donkeys milling in panicky circles due to some threat or crisis, while a large, gimpy, useless human yells confusing and largely useless commands. Rose has faced such challenges many times by now, on my farm and others. She puts things right.

There ought to be a trophy for that.

MY WORRY ABOUT ROSE ISN'T HER HERDING STYLE BUT HER PO-tential isolation. Working dogs are not like other dogs. The more tasks she handles on the farm, the fewer things she can do in the rest of the world—ride comfortably in a car, walk the suburbs on a leash, feel at ease in a mall bookstore. We are conditioned to celebrate the remarkable things a dog like Rose can do, less aware of the accompanying sacrifices.

When friends and I are sitting on the lawn or in the meadow—my dogs playing, getting scratched, taking treats—I always look around for Rose. She is usually off at some distance, her head popping up out of the grass, watching, waiting for a signal. Or she's focused on the sheep, if they're within sight. She's rarely off duty.

I have a question I ask people when they visit the farm, a joke, but also a kind of research.

"I have too many dogs," I mock-complain. "Which one do you want?" Then I keep score. In the past year or two, I've probably asked nearly two hundred people, and only two have answered, "Rose." One of those was a vet.

I'm coming to understand: People want dogs to need them, and Rose doesn't appear to qualify. Unlike Clem or Pearl or Izzy, unlike any dog I've ever had, Rose has little interest in people uninvolved with sheep. In her view, they are just taking up space that ought to be occupied by those wearing fleece. Rose doesn't appear troubled, in need of rescue, or interested in cuddling or bonding with humans.

As close as I am to this dog—in many ways, closer to her than to the others—there's a space between us. She rarely sleeps in the same room with me. She's always nearby, and comes to visit me regularly, but rarely sits on the couch with me or wants to be stroked and petted.

Rose has a mystery of the spirit that I doubt I'll ever penetrate, and perhaps I shouldn't. A part of her remains unreachable. Her fidelity and attachment are evident: What border collie would not love the person who brings her to sheep? But at times, she is a stranger, even to me.

She does reciprocate, though. If training dogs at its purest is about showing them how to live in the world, Rose has helped teach me how to live in mine. As is often the case with dogs, unwitting partners in our dramas, I don't believe Rose does this work for me knowingly or consciously.

Affectionate moments between Rose and me are largely private. Once in a while when she's out watching the sheep in the meadow across the street, she will break off, skitter up to me, lick me furiously about the face, then turn and run back.

Even though she doesn't follow me from room to room, she does check up on me. Every morning, when Winston begins crowing, just before first light, Rose hops up onto the bed, licks my hand or face, and then disappears. Every now and then she comes and lingers long enough that I can scratch the top of her head or massage her back, two responses she appreciates.

When I fall, which happens too often, especially in winter, she rushes to my side, and barks and nips at my ears until I get up. She will not leave me lying there to go off and sniff deer scat, like some dogs I could mention. Once, when I fell on the ice behind the big barn in the winter, I was tempted to yell, "Rose, go get help. Go down to the Harringtons and tell them to call Anthony." I could almost picture her doing it.

Rose is a hero to me. I admire and respect her. Her work is a daily miracle; she is the indispensable dog. I could not imagine life on the farm without her. Yet more and more, her aloneness touches me.

Perhaps I have been negligent, allowing her to become too disconnected from the world. Or maybe, as I've come to believe, this is part of an inevitable trade-off, the kind that humans face every day. Rose lives the life of a working dog, and that crowds out other things.

It is in some ways a selfish bargain, framed by me, paid for by her. But it is also a timeless role for humans and dogs, powerful and satisfying because it evokes the birth of the historic relationship between our two species.

In many ways I was surprised to realize one recent morning, as we headed wordlessly up into the pasture together, that Rose is not a pet anymore. In that, there's both loss and gain for the pair of us.

Annie, farm goddess

SEVEN

Farm Goddess

ANNIE AND I WERE WALKING TOGETHER TO THE BARNYARD TO FILL the water tubs when she gave a little sigh. "Sometimes," she said, "my life seems to revolve around goat penises."

Announcements like that pop out of Annie's mouth from time to time. Still, the line left me somewhat speechless. I wasn't sure whether to inquire further.

Annie looked abashed. "Oh, don't think I'm a freak," she said. And then, "Well, I suppose I am a freak. It's just that with nine goats, some of them going in and out of heat, you have to stay aware of things. Else you get humped, butted, or mounted all the time. You know, whenever there are males, there is trouble."

I barely knew Annie DiLeo a year ago; today she is one of

the most important people in my life. It's hard to imagine Bedlam Farm without her.

Annie's a former construction worker—fit, buff, blond, in her early forties—and a refugee from the crowded suburbs downstate.

Like many such immigrants, she was powerfully drawn to nature and to the elemental, emotional relationships people can form with animals. It was her dream to have a farm populated by animals of all kinds. Much of her life already revolved around a cat, some chickens, a pig, and, especially, her goats.

After two and a half years spent struggling to run the farm pretty much by myself, I'd hired Annie to bail me out. She was strong, had nearly inexhaustible energy, and remained invariably genial and cheerful, albeit with a dark sense of humor. Under the baseball caps she always wore, her bright hair hung to her shoulders.

There was also something vulnerable, though not delicate, about her, as if she expected to be criticized or treated harshly and was a bit surprised when she wasn't.

I asked Annie if she liked the title farm manager, and she said she preferred Bedlam Farm Goddess. This worked out neatly: She badly needed a job; I urgently required a Farm Goddess.

Annie could handle herself. You never had to wonder what she was thinking; if you gave her any guff, you got it right back.

"You're fired" was my greeting several mornings a week. "You forgot to fill the water tub."

"The benefits were lousy anyway," she'd say.

Although officially its goddess, she was the farm's advocate as well, monitoring its animals and barns and grounds—and its protector. Annie looked out for me, staring down uninvited visitors, keeping me supplied, tracking the state of my cranky back.

I have made few unequivocally brilliant moves in life. Marrying Paula was one. Fathering Emma. Buying the farm, as they say. And Annie.

She's one of those people who has occasionally struggled to deal with people—"especially men," she admits—but who loves animals so wholeheartedly that caring for them has become a significant part of her life, a vocation she has almost unconsciously slipped into.

"Animals are so easy to bring pleasure to," she told me when we first sat on my front porch steps on a chilly spring day and talked about her working on the farm. "They are grateful for whatever you give them, and they love you unconditionally."

She studied animals, watched them, thought about them, imagined their conversations and emotions and interactions. She was forever telling me that a donkey was discouraged, a dog eager for play, a cow in need of cuddling. She always knew which resident was nervous, hungry, or sore.

WHEN I CONSIDERED OFFERING HER THE JOB, I NEVER DOUBTED Annie's generosity of spirit or capacity for hard work. But I was concerned that we had divergent philosophies about animal care. She loved all animals; I appreciated some more than others. She would nurse any animal, trying to keep it alive as long as possible; I wouldn't. She would give refuge to as many animals as a given homestead could sustain; I was vigilant about maintaining balance.

She freely personified animals, attributing all sorts of complex emotions, motives, and behaviors to sheep and hens and especially dogs. I try to avoid that.

I drew sharp lines. The barn cat, the dogs, and, to some extent, the donkeys and the steer were companions, pets. Everything else was livestock.

I won't give or sell my lambs to people who want to bring them into their kitchens, for example, and nurse them with bottles like babies. To me it feels disturbing, something that may make humans feel good but that disrupts the natural order of things. Annie made no such distinctions.

Perhaps that's because Annie has an extraordinary ability to communicate with pigs and goats, sheep and donkeys. Each morning, she greets each animal by name—"Hello, Jeannette, you look hungry." "Morning, Clem, is that a tick on your head?" I believe Annie is one of those people, written about for thousands of years, with special gifts enabling her to connect with animals' spirits. I am not so blessed, although I feel quite attuned to my dogs and donkeys.

So when we talked about her working on the farm, I warned that we might have conflicts about running the farm and managing the welfare of its inhabitants.

I will have the vet put down a sick sheep that's unlikely to recover with simple treatment, for instance. If a ewe is suffering and the vet can't come immediately, I'll shoot her myself. I don't want sick animals on my farm, and there are limits to what I will spend on sheeps' health (though few, if any, on my dogs').

Animals that behave aggressively or inappropriately, I get rid of. Increasingly, the farm—capital F—comes first. No single resident is more important.

I could see Annie's eyes widen as I explained. Annie would think nothing of taking a chicken home for a week to nurse a wound. She'll stop for a snake or possum hit by a car, nurse a baby bird that's fallen from its nest. She's prepared organic grains and baked homemade treats for goats, donkeys, and sheep. But she's also a direct person who appreciates honesty.

And she'd already seen our differences in action. For a few weeks last spring, I had two goats I hoped would help chew down the barnyard brush and weeds to manageable levels. They were pesky, bright, needy, and, it turned out, not for me. They developed bad infections from a botched dehorning, and Annie came by two or three times a day for two weeks to nurse their wounds, keep the flies and maggots away, apply antibiotics, teach the goats to run and play.

I couldn't get the goats to sit still for a minute, yet they crawled into Annie's lap while she performed messy, painstaking ministrations. I disliked their bleating and worried about their numerous attempts to vault fences. When they recovered, I sent them home with Annie to join her cadre, where it was clear they'd be happier.

So I marveled at her nurturing instincts, but I also worried about them. Annie was definitely a troubled-animal magnet. I suspect she emits some secret signal that attracts stray cats and dogs, unwanted goats, even rabbits to her door. She was forever finding animals, healing them, then finding homes for them.

I didn't want the farm filling up with rescued animals who would, under Annie's loving care, live forever.

I was also worried that Annie would be so drawn to the animals that she might neglect the rest of the farm, recently expanded to 110 acres. Her duties would involve the more taxing jobs that I could no longer tackle because of my back—hauling hay, laying hoses, tending to electric fences, maintaining the gardens.

She'd have to shovel out manure from the barns, tote extra

hay to Elvis, collect debris, roll out garbage cans, move firewood from the barns to the porch, where I could reach it. A lot of work, only some of it involving animal care.

Annie took in my concerns but seemed untroubled by what she was hearing. "Let's see what happens," she said. "I love the farm and I'd love to work here."

AS IT TURNED OUT, ABSOLUTELY NONE OF MY FEARS WERE JUSTIFIED.

Annie pulled up in her pickup around seven each morning, brought the cat some treat or another, then checked the hay feeders and water tubs. I heard her cheerful greetings as she said hello to Mother and Elvis and Winston, to the sheep, chickens, and donkeys. Often she took the dogs for longer walks than I could manage, through the woods or down to the creek below the meadow.

She might spend half the day if fences needed tending or there was a lot of garden work to do, or if I were limping badly. At such times, she would simply take charge, feeding the dogs, moving firewood around, even doing some shopping so that I had food. But usually, she was here in the morning and again at dusk, and went off to tend her own menagerie in between.

The plan was that I would take care of the farm myself on weekends. I'd do the sheepherding and house chores. I would also, I hoped, have time to write.

It worked from the beginning. Though we might feel differently about animal boundaries, she respected human ones. She never came near my office when I was working. She could be outside, mucking barns or weed-whacking along the fence lines, and I wouldn't even know it. She had a relentless appetite for work, but also that rare capacity to be at ease within herself, without needing to chat or interact.

From the first, she worked as hard (well, almost) to understand me, my moods, and my values as to care for Jeannette or Rupert. She knew that I needed time alone, that I couldn't concentrate if the dogs weren't fed and exercised, that there were some physical tasks I simply could no longer manage.

For instance, I never told Annie that it was painful for me to climb on and off the ATV, which I do twenty times a day, to take Rose or Izzy out to practice herding, or take the sheep to graze. I pull the ATV up to a pasture gate, climb off, open or close the gate, climb back on the ATV, then repeat the process, a series of motions hard on my touchy back. A few days after Annie came to work here, though, I would pull up to a gate and find it already opened. When I came back through, I would turn around and it would be closed.

A small thing, really, but not so small. I was able to sit down to work earlier and work longer. I felt better; I could do more. I sometimes laughed to myself that I might well become one of Annie's ailing creatures, nurtured lovingly beyond my natural life span. If such care was okay for me, why not for a sheep?

We would, I suspected, wind up changing each other a bit.

Annie has known challenge and sadness almost all her life. She had a painful childhood she can barely speak about. And a decade ago, the man she was about to marry was killed in a motorcycle accident. "I do know that sometimes, for me, the animals are standing in for the suffering of people," she told me one morning, as she joined me in taking the sheep out to pasture.

Annie's ability to communicate with animals is so powerful that, as a Christmas gift, I bought her some study sessions with a friend, an animal communicator and shaman in Vermont.

But her love of animals—and theirs for her—has already significantly reshaped the farm. Its population is more peaceful, more content, markedly more social than before she came.

When my rooster Winston lay near death on the barn floor last winter, and I was heading to the house to get my rifle and mercifully end his life, Annie swooped in, picked him up, warmed him, administered special potions and food, and brought him back to life before my eyes, shocking several friends and farmers. He had a rough couple of weeks, but Winston crows every morning, still.

When Rose and I take the sheep out to pasture every morning, Mother, the barn cat, sits at the edge of the meadow and watches us. She won't approach me when Rose is nearby. When Annie joins us, though, Mother comes sprinting across the pasture, purring excitely, to wrap herself around Annie's feet.

I'm not close to many of my sheep, but they'll come rushing up to Annie so she can scratch their chins and rub their noses.

I'm fond of Jesus, the baby donkey, and he always comes up to me to be patted. But when he sees Annie, he canters over in visible joy, nibbling on her shoes and pants legs, following her around.

Even Rose, normally so restrained, is crazy about Annie and will dash off to walk with her and sit nearby when there's work to do in the garden.

Of course, Annie has her own ways. One day, hearing the dogs going crazy, I looked out the window to see her walking up the driveway with her favorite Nubian goat, Midas, trotting alongside her like a show dog at the Westminster Kennel Club trials. I came out, surprised, and a bit irritated. "Yo!" I bellowed from the porch. "This isn't a zoo!" Unfazed, Annie explained that she just liked bringing Midas along sometimes. He followed her while she put hay in the feeder, crossed the road with her while she fed Mother, and stood by while she brushed the donkeys.

When I thought about it, Midas wasn't harming or bothering anyone. If it made Annie happy once in a while, why not? But I cautioned her about doing it too often; the farm *wasn't* a zoo.

I shouldn't have been surprised. Annie's idea of a great time is to go with her husband, Joe, a trucker and logger, to the Saturday-night livestock auction.

When she showed up one Monday morning, my dogs came thundering out and surrounded her. Pearl, Izzy, Rose, and Clem always greeted Annie enthusiastically—Annie is nothing but good news to a dog—but this cluster seemed more intense than usual.

Then I noticed her jacket pocket moving. "What's that?"

"Oh," she said, "I almost forgot." And she pulled out a baby rabbit, all white, about the size of a teacup. "This is Eli. We bought him at the auction for Joe."

She wore a small carrying case over one shoulder, in which Eli would spend the next few hours, she explained, and in which he would travel.

I was concerned about Eli's proximity to four intense herding and hunting dogs, all circling and eyeing him with noticeable passion. All four are ferocious stalkers of small creatures in the woods and have tangled with chipmunks, squirrels, moles, rabbits, even raccoons.

"Forget it, Pearl," Annie said. "Rose, don't even think about it. Izzy, no way. Clem, back off, this isn't a chew toy." One by one, Annie calmed the dogs, and they drifted off to other pursuits. To me, it was a miracle that the rabbit had lived through the encounter.

I got a bit stuffy and for a while considered banning Annie's animals from the farm. Was this really the tone I wanted to set, having odd rabbits and goats parading around the place? It seemed undignified.

But her animals are a huge part of Annie's life, and she's become a critical part of mine. Who else could I leave a dog like Rose with and not worry for a second? If anybody else tried to take Izzy for a walk, he would run back to look for me, but he trotted off with Annie without a second thought.

And then there was the cow. The farm animal I'd grown closer to than any other was Elvis, strangely enough. Somehow I just connected with this monster, whose size and erratic movements unnerved most people. Even Annie had gotten smacked when he swung his massive head.

When Elvis arrived, accustomed to sleeping on a concrete barn floor, he had chunks of hardened manure stuck to his haunches. Annie worked every day with soap and water and a brush to clean him off; caked manure, to her, was a sign that an animal was not being treated as lovingly as she preferred.

Some elements of livestock care are simply gross—from mucking to administering rectal thermometers to dressing wounds. Annie didn't find any of these tasks repulsive, and the animals—I saw it again and again—simply turned themselves over to her. Soon Elvis's brown hide was clean and elegant.

"Do people laugh at you?" I asked Annie one day while we sat on the porch steps. We were brushing the dogs, checking them over for ticks.

"Yes, I'm sure they do," she said.

"Do they think you're nuts?"

"Oh, yes, of course."

"And it doesn't bother you?"

"Not anymore. I don't care what people think. I love working with animals, caring for them. They are so appreciative. Unlike people. It's so easy to make them happy. So doing things for them is very satisfying."

I never met characters like this in suburbia, but here they were tucked away in the hills and valleys all around: the Jewish donkey spiritualist; the aging Hollywood icon who raises herding dogs; the religious hermit in a nearby town who maintains a vow of silence.

A few years ago, I might have viewed Annie differently. But she doesn't seem nuts to me, not anymore. Increasingly, it's the allegedly normal guys you see bellowing on cable talk shows who strike me as freakish.

Maybe Annie is an aberration of sorts, far from what our culture considers the mainstream. Soccer moms back in New Jersey wouldn't lovingly clean a steer's rump. But they're not Farm Goddesses, a rare and proud species.

My animals, of course, remain unconcerned about any of the labels people like to claim or impose. It's of no concern to them—nor to me, anymore—whether Annie is running toward something or whether she is running away. We all just want her to stay.

Perhaps she is an oddball. Or maybe she has simply found the right circus.

EIGHT

Names and Numbers

IT WAS A FEW WEEKS AFTER ANNIE CAME TO WORK ON THE FARM THAT I noticed a change in the way my sheep were behaving. Usually, when they see Rose, they bunch together and wait, resignedly, to be shuttled to one pasture or another.

But they began rushing up to me and to other people. Sometimes they sniffed at my pockets. A couple of times they ran right around or over the shocked Rose, and it took some nipping and charging to set them straight.

When you work with dogs, this matters. Herding is a complex synergy, involving the movement and temperament of livestock, dogs, and humans. Some say it's one of the most difficult of organized animal activities. It looks pretty simple with a dog as competent as Rose, but it's not.

It works best when the dog and sheep are entirely focused

on one another, when neither is sniffing around humans or otherwise distracted. So when two or three of the ewes suddenly turned balky, ignoring or even butting at Rose, causing her to grow more aggressive in turn, it was disturbing.

What was going on?

I looked out my office window one morning to see Annie reaching into her pockets and offering the sheep, clustered around her, something to eat. I went outside and asked what she'd been feeding them.

"Oh, peanuts," she said. "I always bring some with me for the sheep."

Now I understood. The sheep had begun to associate people with their favorite thing—food—and so paid less attention to the dog. To do her job, therefore, Rosie had to get uncharacteristically rough, a trait I didn't want to encourage.

So Annie and I began our latest—and by no means last—disagreement about animal care. We'd already argued about feeding the dogs food from the table, or from her lunch. We argued about how much time and money should be spent to keep alive a ewe.

Now we jousted about whether it was a good idea to give sheep peanuts.

When it comes to sheep, I have a few I know and feel fond of, and they come up to me for scratches or to angle for some of the snacks I'm taking to the donkeys. There are two or three good mothers I respect. But mostly, their lack of individuality—behaving like a sheep doesn't sound like a compliment to me—and their one-dimensional personalities don't make it easy for me to attach to them.

Some people—including Annie—argue that this is because they only encounter me with a dog. So I regard them from a border collie perspective, and they associate me with canine training. Could be true. But I have only so much time, money, emotion, and affection to go around, I tell Annie. I have to make choices. Dogs come first, donkeys close behind, then the steer, then sheep, and chickens.

I could lie and say I love all my animals equally, but then that would be . . . well, a lie. It cost well over a thousand dollars for Pearl's multiple surgeries to repair her damaged ligaments. I wouldn't spend that on a ewe. When Izzy or Rose is sick, we rush to the vet. With other animals, I wait a bit to see how they fare. My pantry is crammed with treats, chews, and toys for the dogs. I've never brought treats to sheep, although I bring the donkeys cookies and Elvis gets his daily apples.

I treat the flock well, provide the best food, freshest water, safest fences. I protect them from predators with my donkeys, give them their shots and deworming medication.

But I've always been clear about why they're here: to be herded by border collies.

THE SHEEP EPITOMIZE THE NAMES-VERSUS-NUMBERS CULTURES OF animal care around me. Often, when I call the large-animal vets, the dispatcher asks if my animals have names or numbers. It puzzled me, until experience and observation clarified the practice.

People who name their animals see them as individual personalities and are much more likely to attribute human-like emotions to them. I would never put a tag in Pearl's ear and call her Number 12. But farmers can't afford to personify animals, so they give them numbers.

Vets know that animals with numbers are apt to be "production animals"—headed for market. Farmers won't spend more on their care than the animal is worth; if the treatment cost exceeds the market price, the animal is likely to be euthanized.

Whereas animals with names—not only dogs and horses but some sheep, goats, and alpacas—are seen as individuals, sometimes even family members. Their owners are far more likely to spend what it takes to make them well.

Some vets only treat animals with numbers, others only animals with names. Asking about nomenclature is as good a system as any for letting them know what kind of care people will pay for.

My dogs and donkeys have names. So does Elvis (and Mother). But only four of my sheep do. Paula is the first ewe we bought, and I named her after my wife. Brutus is her good-natured son, a wether (neutered male). I named both rams. But my favorite ewe is called Number 57.

Two years ago, Number 57 gave birth to healthy twin lambs, and in the melee of sorting the sheep being sold to another farmer from the sheep that were staying, I mistakenly sent her lambs away. It was awful. She was the best, most conscientious mother in the flock, and her mournful bleating, though it lasted just two days, haunted me for weeks. I bred the sheep again the next year, in some measure to give Number 57 another shot at motherhood.

She's the only one in the flock that has fought past the dogs to get to know me, who shows individual personality traits. Number 57 comes trotting over to me, skittering around Rose to get her nose scratched and take a donkey cookie or carrot if I offer. She has a black face and big bright eyes; as with Elvis, it seems to me something is going on in there. Perhaps that's also true of the other ewes; the truth is, I don't have the time, or need, to find out. Rose, seeing that I welcome her visits, gives Number 57 a pass.

So it was particularly odd, in early March, that Number 57 began charging at Rose when we entered the pasture, butting, even kicking her. Rose could not back her off or keep her at bay, nor could she get her to join the rest of the herd. It went on for five or six increasingly testy days, as Rose grew more focused on this ewe and began using her mouth to defend herself and to try to move 57.

I called the vet, who came and checked her out. "She's fine," he said. "Nothing wrong with her." So I isolated her for two days, then let her out—and she went right at Rose again.

"I think I may have to shoot her or have her put down," I told Annie. "This just isn't healthy. She may be getting old or grumpy." I didn't want her turning Rose into a hunting dog instead of a herding dog; we'd worked too hard for that. One morning, I warned Annie, Number 57 just might not be here.

Annie, horrified, disagreed. I soon heard from friends that she was frantically calling around, trying to find a new home for 57.

Soon afterward, riding up the pasture on the ATV to take another look, I saw with chagrin the reason for the out-of-character behavior. It was ridiculously simple: Number 57 was lying down with Jesus, the newborn donkey. A vigilant mother, even if the baby wasn't hers, she was trying to stay between him and Rose.

I told Annie she didn't have to find a new home for 57; the ewe was more than welcome to stay. In a week or two, I suspected, 57 would relax and calm down and let Rose do her job. Sure enough, in a few days, she and Rose had worked things out and herding returned to normal.

Annie told me she didn't really believe that I would have killed my favorite ewe. I think I could have, and in the event of future problems, I would. In the meantime, whether she or any of these sheep were benefiting from regular doses of peanuts was still under discussion.

AND IT WASN'T THE ONLY DEBATE. AS I ACQUIRED BOTH KINDS OF animals, the named and the numbered, my ideas about how to treat and train them evolved. I had little choice.

Four dogs is a lot, especially when combined with the other creatures. Somebody was always bleeding, puking, limping, chewing something forbidden, needing limits set or behavior modified. They were all great dogs, and I felt lucky to have each one. But sometimes I had to confront issues quickly and decisively, mixing numbered approaches with the named kind.

Izzy, the new border collie, was a breathtakingly agile escape artist. Like many older dogs who finally find a human to latch on to, he was anxious to locate me all the time. He dug under fences and jumped over gates, pushing aside obstructions. Several times he came roaring into the pasture when Rose and I were herding, panicking the animals and causing some potentially dangerous situations—ewes plowing into fences, Elvis stampeding in manic circles, donkeys jostling me.

To follow me on the ATV, he once vaulted a gate and took off down the road, narrowly avoiding a passing car. Anthony saw him carefully lift a chain with his teeth and open the dog pen. Izzy was going to get hurt, either by his attempts to break out or by what could happen to him when he succeeded.

It was a similar dilemma with Elvis, who could push through any fence if he took a mind to, that led me to consider a new tack with Izzy.

If electrifying a fence could teach a cow to stay put, could it do the same for a wild-eyed border collie?

The mass marketing of shock collars for dogs—notice the

variety of devices sold at any pet store chain—is disturbing. Sometimes, I acknowledge, shock collars and electric fences can be appropriate, sensible, and useful, preventing dogs from getting hurt or attacking other dogs or people. But they make me uneasy.

I would rather train a dog into a behavior than shock him, while many busy people shock first. Why bother to train a dog when you can just zap him? Done casually or thoughtlessly, shocks can spook a dog. The relationship can become one of fear rather than partnership.

Yet a dog like Izzy—easily aroused, full of ferocious energy and drive and working instincts, but with no training at all for the first three years of his life—generated almost constant mayhem. I had to be vigilant about letting him stay inside the yard or back fence, since neither could reliably hold him—a problem because there were so many visitors, so much construction, so many opportunities for him to get injured.

A few years ago, I would have spent half the day sitting with him in the yard, repeating "sit" and "stay" or "lie down" several hundred times, rewarding him for being calm. But that would take months or years, and even then, with a dog this excitable, might only be intermittently successful. So I had Annie rig up a fence charger at the gates to the back fence and to the front yard, the two places where Izzy most frequently escaped. I then took Rose up into the pasture to get the sheep—Izzy was always desperate to come along—and turned off the ATV and waited.

I watched Izzy race toward the front gate and heard a sharp yelp. Poor Annie was distressed at having to resort to this tactic—"He's been through so much"—but after years of border collie chess, my heart had hardened. "Yes!" I yelled. "Got you, you little SOB."

Then I ATV'd down the hill and around to the yard. Izzy

was sitting a foot from the gate, staring quizzically. He didn't seem frightened or disoriented. He is a stoic, like others of his breed. But he's also smart. It took one more zap, and Izzy has never escaped from a fence since. After a precautionary couple of weeks, we removed the wire.

This was a strategy I wouldn't have employed a couple of years ago. But Izzy didn't get harmed and he avoided months of getting yelled at. He accepted what all good working dogs must learn to accept, quietly if not happily: Sometimes it's their turn, sometimes it isn't. Rose may whimper a bit when she has to watch Izzy herd her sheep, but then she lies quietly and waits. She always gets her turn. Izzy now does the same.

This simple procedure—it took a few minutes, and cost about thirty dollars—changed the nature of my life with Izzy, a shocking notion in itself. Dogs love routines, boundaries, and rules, once they understand what they are. It almost seemed that once Izzy grasped that he couldn't escape, he was relieved of the burden of having to try. It was a significant step for both of us.

I'm still not a fan of the shock collar. Had I put one on this dog and zapped him every time he went near the gate or street, I think I might have driven him mad with anxiety and confusion. Zaps coming out of nowhere, I believe, are harder for the dog to understand and avoid. Working dogs are genetically programed to succeed, and their spirits can be crushed by failure and criticism. But fences and gates represent a clear, simple boundary.

I'd spent years trying to train Orson out of habits like these through a rigid adherence to positive reinforcement—praising desired behaviors, ignoring undesired ones. It was a protracted and difficult process, and ultimately it failed. The fault was mine, not the method's. Yet I wasn't sure I had enough patience to see if the method would work with another older, untrained border collie; I wasn't sure Izzy had enough time.

While I still adhere to the philosophy of positive reinforcement, I've also learned the value of confronting dangerous or problematic behaviors squarely, then putting them behind the dog and the human.

I've learned the hard way that this is an animal, albeit a smart and loved one, governed by instincts, boundaries, and habits. The fright and hurt of the shock would pass much more quickly than getting hit by a car. And my bet was that Izzy wouldn't leap a fence again.

As was often the case with names versus numbers, I found myself drifting more often into the middle ground, finding my own blend of approaches and attitudes.

With my furry Houdini safely confined, I had more freedom, felt less anxious, less vigilant. The dog could also relax and avoid behavior that brought rebukes. Instead of spending months working to rechannel a behavior, we simply stopped it. And we could both move on to happier activities like herding sheep, riding ATVs, and hanging out together. He was great at all of that.

BUT BACK TO THE QUESTION OF SHEEP AND PEANUTS.

In general, farm animals don't need treats.

The donkeys appreciate the carrots and cookies I offer them, but they don't rush the gate to get them. After a quick snack, they go off about their business.

Elvis needed some kind of training because of his staggering size. Apples had proved an incentive that could get him to move when necessary, or to stop moving.

But the sheep were so obsessively food-driven that they would plow right into or over me and one another for a cup of grain. Why encourage them to charge at people? They got grain, plenty of hay and water, plus salt blocks and mineral licks. They had ample pasture to graze. Why did they need peanuts?

But when Annie showed up with a pocketful one morning while I was out preparing to herd, she handed me some peanuts.

"Here," she said. "Give it a try." She'd evidently been waiting for the right moment to launch this experiment.

I held out a nut and one ewe—Number 72—immediately trotted over and took it, munching until she'd cracked the shell. She liked it, so I gave her another. Pretty soon the whole flock was pressing around us as we distributed peanuts. Rupert, the new ram, seemed especially fond of them. I scratched his chin, and he nearly purred.

"It's a good thing," said Annie. "It relaxes them, gives them a good feeling about people. And it makes you feel good, too. I can tell."

Well, sort of. I was pleased that the flock might come to associate me with something other than a work-obsessed border collie.

And I understood that the script called for me to see the light, and bring these sheep into the emotional circle that the dogs and donkeys had entered. Yet I resisted.

The sheep don't need peanuts, I told Annie. In some ways—because it led them to charge or pester humans, thus riling the dogs—it was unhealthy as well as unnecessary, one of those things that make us feel better but don't really bring a healthier, more pleasurable or meaningful life to the animals.

I wanted to maintain certain boundaries. Apart from herding, shearing, and vet visits, I was just as happy to let the sheep go their way while I went mine. I didn't want these animals to move closer to the center of my emotional life, already a slightly crowded realm. I didn't care to expend more time, money, or energy than necessary to keep them healthy and content. There's a line; peanuts seemed a bit over it.

Yet I'd learned to take Annie's notions about animal care seriously, and I wanted her to know that how she felt was important, because it was. My own ideas were evolving at the same time.

What if occasional peanuts might brighten a sheep's world a bit and, in the process, our own?

"How about giving them peanuts every couple of weeks?" I suggested. Not so often that they stampeded toward us whenever we approached, just now and again?

"Fine with me," Annie said. I went to get Rose.

Here was a creature unambivalent about how to treat sheep. She bolted through the gate and into the pasture. Rupert put his head down and charged. She was soon hanging off his butt, and he fled into the center of the flock.

A couple of ewes took a few steps toward me, to see if I had any more peanuts. Rose seemed highly annoyed at these breaches of decorum. In a flash, all the sheep—ram included— were in a tight circle, moving briskly toward the pasture.

Another minute and they were spread out in a line, grazing contentedly under Rose's supervision. This was the picture that seemed right to me.

Clementine

NINE

Whore of Bedlam

A RECENT VISITOR LOOKED SURPRISED WHEN I INTRODUCED Clementine as "the Whore of Bedlam Farm." It wasn't the sort of terminology she associated with beloved dogs.

"What a terrible thing to call her," she scolded. "And she's such a sweetie."

It's true, Clem is a sweetie. And no one loves her more than I do. But the truth is the truth.

We have a little debate going about this. A prostitute is someone who sells his or her favors, and this dog will give it up—anytime, anywhere—for a sliver of beef jerky. My wife, however, argues that Clem is more accurately a slut. Clem loves everyone, free of charge, Paula points out; Clem gives it away, even without beef jerky. But I'm convinced that food is key.

Clementine may be the most loving dog I've ever had, viscerally and inherently affectionate. She's technically a hunting dog, but unless you count squeaky toys, this predatory trait has yet to surface. Instead, for a piece of hamburger, she will climb into your car, cuddle with you in bed, and probably move into your house.

What else but a whore would you call a dog who hops into the UPS truck after glimpsing the biscuit box beneath the dashboard?

What would you call a dog who rushes into a vet's examining room, hops eagerly onto the table, slurps the vet and wags throughout injections and rectal temperature-taking, the whole time staring at the treat jar on the counter?

As the ur-Labrador, embodying the best traits of the breed—affection, loyalty, sociability, contemplation, an interest in (occasional) work—Clem also has other, less appealing habits.

If border collies test human patience with their obsessive busyness and need to work, Labs test the limits of our tolerance for revolting smells, messes, and dead animals. Try living with two Labs on a farm surrounded by woods. Clem loves chicken feed, donkey and sheep droppings, the carcasses of the mice and rats that Mother slays. The longer something has been dead, the more pungent the fecal matter, the muckier and smellier the mud bog, the more likely she is to find it, roll in it, rub her face in it, and, for good measure, shower you with it as she shakes herself off.

Like many foolish people with Labs, I spend a lot of time yelling, "Hey, drop that!" or "No, put it down!" Clem looks at me curiously, chews a bit, sometimes drops the gross thing, sometimes not. I wouldn't care much, except that what goes in comes out in even less pleasant form; Clem is the cover girl for those odor and stain removers.

If you have a border collie and do your job, you will learn patience. If you have Labs, you will learn to stretch the boundaries of hygiene. I'm told that the original Labs hailed not from Labrador but from Newfoundland, where they worked with tough and tired fishermen who let them hang around but didn't provide organic or vegan dog food. As a result, Labs became scavengers, with little fussiness about what they ate.

Yet the trade-off is worthwhile. I have a loving dog I can trust completely around human beings. A neighbor's two-year-old crawled across the kitchen floor last year toward Clementine's food bowl—before Clem had finished her supper. It was foolish of me not to be paying closer attention, but when I turned and realized what was happening, I saw the toddler sampling the kibble and Clem sitting nearby, wagging her tail, looking aggrieved but resigned.

That's worth a lot of mudbaths to me. Dogs should not hurt people, even for understandable reasons, and a well-bred Lab will do almost anything to avoid harming a human. I can't conceive of her attacking anyone (including, surely, any burglar entering the house).

This spring, Clem's day begins with a walk in the woods and some ball-chasing. Then she and Pearl sun themselves in the yard while the border collies race around like fools with the sheep.

Then a lunchtime walk, and sometimes a ride around town on errands. Clem gets her own private ball-chasing session—she has great stamina and focus, runs far, always gets her ball and brings it back faithfully and efficiently. I usually take her out to the barn for the last round of chores, and she greets the donkeys and other animals with her usual equanimity, gravitating to her favorite spots—piles of manure. Then she's done for the day, crawling onto a couch or collapsing on her dog bed on the porch.

She will chase the occasional chipmunk, but more for form than function, as if she were showing Rose and Izzy that she's one of the guys. Aside from the time she swallowed a bumblebee (with no ill effect) that flew too close, I've never seen her harm a living thing.

As a bird dog, she ought not to be fond of the hens or delighted to see Winston. But she's as affectionate as she is indiscriminate. All things bring her joy, though things wrapped in supermarket plastic probably top the list. Which is why I got her and, of course, why I love her to pieces.

There are different ways to love a dog. I love Izzy for his complexity, for his resilience; he's slowly filling the opening for soulmate. Rose is my working partner and protector. Pearl fulfilled a need to heal and be healed. But I love Clem because—well, if you have a pulse, you have to love Clem.

There's a One True Love notion in the dog world, the conviction that a dog attaches itself to you and only you. It's potent. At one gathering where I was speaking, a woman chastised me for not believing that dogs mourn their people for years, sometimes forever. She knew a dog whose owner had died, and the dog pined on and on, she insisted, moping for his person, watching his closet, staring at the space where his car used to be parked, searching and scanning for his return. "How can you say they don't have complex feelings?" this woman said, disappointed, even a bit angry.

I understand the mythology. A town in Scotland has erected a statue of a border collie who came to the train station every day, looking for his master, for nearly a decade after the man died. This is the mythic version of dog devotion we want so much to believe. Sometimes, perhaps, it's even true.

So I presented the never-fail Clementine Demonstration of Canine Attachment: I took a bag of biscuits from my pants pocket and handed it to the woman. "Now shake the bag," I instructed, "and call Clem."

All it took was the crinkle of plastic. Clementine awakened from a sound sleep—she'd been snoring at my feet—and popped up as if a gun had been fired. She locked on to the woman and trotted over to her, wagging.

"Now walk out the door, open your car, and get in," I said. "Then come back and tell us what happens."

She left the room, Clementine close behind.

When she returned a few minutes later, she reported that Clem had trailed her out into the parking lot and jumped into the car after her. I had no doubt Clem would have gone home with her to score a few biscuits. At some point, she would likely notice that I wasn't there and look around for me and for the other dogs. But within a week, if the food and treats kept coming, she probably would have made her peace in this new place.

"She doesn't seem to be mourning me much," I said.

I sounded cynical, perhaps, but I didn't feel that way. This is an elemental lesson in anybody's life with dogs: There is some slut in almost every canine. They are loving, but they are also bribable. If they were politicians, we'd see a steady stream of indictments.

The Whore of Bedlam makes no pretense about this, but we love each other no less. In fact, accepting her as the delightfully corrupt animal she is improves our relationship. I don't want to love a dog that doesn't exist. I want to recognize what she is, not fantasize about what I want or need her to be.

Who among us doesn't cherish the idea of being loved unconditionally, uncritically, eternally? Something in many of us—from watching too many episodes of *Lassie* and *Rin-Tin-Tin* maybe—needs to believe that dogs love only us, forever.

Learning that this is not really possible—not from an animal—is a fundamental lesson. Clem is under no pressure to be human-like in her affections.

Dogs do miss their absent owners, I'm sure, but we can't know if that means mourning or feeling nervous, wondering about the rules, or simply acting out of habit. They're loyal and uncritical, but . . . flexible.

I can tell you with a light heart that Clementine loves me a lot. And she will love you a lot, too, if you have a hot dog in your hand, or even if you don't. Her love of people—just about all people—is not an act of disloyalty, but the very quality I most treasure about her.

PEOPLE LIKE TO RECOUNT HOW THEIR DOGS "CHOSE" THEM, BUT dogs don't make those kinds of choices; we do. We're the responsible parties. I chose each of my dogs, though I didn't always grasp the underlying reason at the time.

With Clementine, I did know the reason: I wanted to see if, through a first-rate breeder and my own intensive homework and observation, I could choose and train the sort of dog I wanted.

I bought her from the best breeder I've ever met, Pam Leslie of Hillside Labradors in Pawlet, Vermont, though only after months of nagging, cajoling, and flat-out bribery with chocolates and other goodies. Pam, who has been breeding Labs for decades, wasn't easy. Like most good breeders, she doesn't initially trust anybody who wants one of her dogs. It took six months before she would even take my deposit. I swear Pam glowered right up to the minute I hauled tiny Clem away in my arms.

Determined to do right by her, I was present right after her birth, visited the litter almost weekly as I made my choice, hand-fed her, socialized her intensely, loved her madly. I was eager to test my ideas about choosing the right dog and about training. I also felt we could all use some lightening up.

In this scenario, Clementine is as much a working dog as Rose. I can't say what she sensed when she came to Bedlam. Perhaps her well-bred nature kicked in and she came to understand the role I had in mind. In any case, she slipped into it easily.

Clem lives surrounded by intense creatures. I stumble and bumble around all day, doing chores, taking calls, answering e-mail, trying to write, taking care of the animals, fussing about the gazillion details of farm life.

Rose, far more intense than I, waits day or night for work, staring at my shoes to see which boots I'm putting on, noticing which door I go to and whether I grab my shepherd's crook. Rose doesn't stop to sniff the roses. Orson was a bundle of manic energy vigilantly defending his turf. Izzy has settled down nicely, herding sheep in the morning, dashing alongside the ATV, finally forgoing his Houdini escape routines—yet I always keep at least one wary eye on him.

Clementine changed us all. I smile whenever I look at this dog, and I swear she smiles back. All day long, she brings me gifts: gnawed-on rawhide, raggedy remnants of plush toys, dead frogs. But those aren't the gifts that really count.

Lots of times, in the life of a farm, you don't need a dog as busy and intense as Rose—like when you want to brush donkeys or feed chickens or just sit on the porch and read.

At such moments, Clementine is a true champion, as devoted and competent as any dog that ever strutted at Westminster. The donkeys are cautious of Rose due to their tiffs over who controls the sheep, and of the newcomer Izzy. But they have no fear of Clem, even if, uninvited, she shares their oats. When I brush them, she plops down near their feet and dozes. I especially enjoy this quality of hers, the way she cools out nearby when I stop to talk to someone, putter about the barn, take a phone call. She instinctively hits pause to accommodate my needs.

When I am weary or distracted and want to walk or ride up the hill to the Adirondack chairs with the spectacular view, Clem is the dog to bring. Rose cannot be still for that long; Pearl can, but finds the trek difficult; Izzy is still getting there. But when I open a book, or sip a mug of coffee, Clem slips under the chair, stares out over the valley, and goes to sleep.

At night, she curls up next to me on the couch while I watch baseball or read or talk to friends on the phone. She sleeps at the foot of my bed, sometimes making a run at the pillow before being rebuffed. She has the particular gift—less natural to border collies—of being near you without invading your space.

The household has loosened up because of her easygoing presence. Through her, the other dogs discovered, or rediscovered, play. Once Clem began working on her, Rose learned to wrestle, play tug-of-war, and instigate games of hide-and-seek.

Izzy has become visibly more affectionate toward her, week by week. He now tolerates things from Clem I doubt he would have put up with from any other dog—allowing her to lick his empty bowl or finish off his bones.

Another fringe benefit: I don't have to drag Rose to public events anymore—she dislikes them—because Clem is delighted to go. The Whore of Bedlam Farm has also become its ambassador. She's a born greeter; Wal-Mart could hire her.

Kids from the town come up regularly to see her, shouting, "Hey, Clem." She's a simpler dog to comprehend than border collies, and she's also more interested in them, eager to make contact. Such dogs do a lot of good for other dogs.

Once or twice a week, I still drive her down the road to Gardenworks, the classy gifts-and-gardening enterprise built out of a working farm. Clem sits in the doorway, as she did when she was a tiny puppy I wanted to socialize, so that she'd become as easy with strangers and hubbub as she has. She was busy chewing and playing then; now she sits rather regally, waiting for visitors and admirers.

We needed this dog, the Bedlam crew. Her tolerance and good-heartedness have warmed us all up, eased tensions, raised the level of fun.

In the late spring, a rescue dog from Virginia arrived for two nights. He was a cattle dog, abandoned outside Charlottesville, whose rear legs had been fractured, possibly by a car. Members of a rescue group were driving him to a new home in New Hampshire; I'd agreed to serve as a transfer point.

He had casts on both rear legs, and when Clem and I went out to the barn to meet and feed him, I expected him to be docile and wary. Instead, hobbling out of his crate, he lunged and pinned her, his teeth at her throat.

I should have been more careful. The last thing I wanted was to see Clem get hurt, or to have to yank an injured dog off her, or worse. But Clem dropped into a submissive position. The rescue dog growled, then released his grip. Clem wagged her tail, licked his nose. The other dog relaxed. He sniffed the food I'd brought and ate it eagerly. Then Clem and I took him for a short walk.

She seemed to have forgotten their early encounter. As she often had with Orson, she simply pretended the aggression never occurred. Perhaps, for her, it hadn't. Maybe her canine mind just couldn't grasp an assault. The cattle dog couldn't romp, of course, but he did pick up her rope-and-ball toy and hang on for a few seconds while she tugged. It was a start.

I won't put Clem in that position again—a strange rescue dog may have suffered trauma that makes its behavior unpredictable—but as so often happens with dogs, the incident was an eye-opener. It's easy to laugh at Clementine's single-minded devotion to food and affection, but her way of defusing the tension reminded me that she is a more complex creature than I sometimes give her credit for.

The UN could use such a diplomat. Clem had virtually defanged Orson, notoriously dominant and ill-tempered. She'd saved Rose from the common fate of the working dog: humorless, joyless obsessiveness. She'd showed the donkeys that some dogs are good to have around. And in the midst of Bedlam, she'd given me an anchor I needed more than I realized.

Archaeologists and anthropologists have found a great deal of evidence of primitive humans' awareness of the ancient intelligence of the dog, their sense of unity with dogs, and their recognition of the mystery of the dog's spirit.

I can joke about Clementine—even call her a whore—but her work is not simple; she just makes it look that way. Her communications skills are profound, effective, far beyond my own. And her affection has proved, time after time, contagious. For all that I see her as simple, I could not defuse Orson on my own, nor lighten Rose up, nor find as many moments as I should to relax and take in the special beauty of my farm.

Orson's neediness led me here, and Rose allows me to stay and care for my extended flock. But Clementine is helping me to appreciate what being here really means, and asking only for a steady supply of microwaved hamburger in return.

Jon with Rose, Pearl, and Clementine

TEN

Citizen of Nowhere

My friends from the city had chosen an unfortunate week-end for their visit. A drenching nor'easter blew in and stayed. The farm was neither beautiful, soothing, nor inspiring; it was rank, disgusting, and depressing.

If you went outside, you sank up to your ankles in mud. If you went into the pasture, you sank further, in worse.

I had to change my clothes and boots two or three times a day. The dogs tracked in muck and transferred it to the rugs and furniture. I hung my vest near the woodstove; it wouldn't dry for days. The old farmhouse, the dampness summoning the effects of countless other storms over nearly two centuries, added its own flavor to the stinky brew.

On Sunday, my friends, getting ready to leave after hours of reading and Scrabble, hugged me at the door, paused outside to pop open the umbrellas they'd brought, then walked the fifteen feet down the driveway to their car—where they closed their umbrellas, dove into the car, waved, and drove off.

A very small incident, of no particular significance. Yet it stuck in my mind, and it took me a while to figure out why.

I called Anthony. "Do you own an umbrella?" I asked.

"A what?"

"An umbrella. For rain."

He'd never used one. He yelled to Holly, who said she thought there might be one in the mudroom.

Then I called my friend Becky, a special-ed teacher who lives nearby; she couldn't remember ever owning an umbrella.

I hadn't used one myself, I realized, since I came to the farm. I wasn't sure I'd even seen one up here. Yet I was out in the weather fifty times a day, rain or shine. In New Jersey, we kept umbrellas by the back door, and used them whenever we walked dogs, headed for the train station, or took out the recycling in a downpour.

Now I pull on a hooded parka and expect to get soaked. Getting wet, cold, or muddy is simply part of living here. A small thing like an umbrella was a symbol of how I'd shifted from one culture to another or, perhaps, vanished into the gulf in between.

IN ALL MY STRUGGLES WITH IDENTITY, BATTLES WITH BOSSES, CHOICES about careers, agonies about direction, I never foresaw that I'd be living on a farm with dogs, sheep, donkeys, cows, and chickens, or would define myself as someone increasingly shaped by farming and animals.

So I can understand why friends and acquaintances keep asking me: Do you fit in here? Are you accepted?

When you move from a city or suburb to a remote hamlet where your occupation, your ethnicity, even the fact that you and your wife have different surnames are all unusual, do you ever feel fully at ease?

My answer is no. But that's because I never fully belong. If I've learned anything about myself and my identity, it's this: I'm an outsider. I don't naturally fit in anywhere.

I was reminded of this somewhat painfully one beautiful spring afternoon. I was across the road with one of the guys working on my barn, unloading some stuff from Annie's truck. A man came speeding down the hill, nearly clipping the truck and us.

The worker yelled to slow down. The driver slammed on the brakes, backed up his truck, and jumped out screaming obscenities. He hit my helper in the face two or three times, bloodying his lip, and when I moved between them, he slugged me, too. Then he jumped into his truck and took off.

I wasn't injured, though my cheek was swollen for an hour or two until an ice pack soothed it, but I was shocked and bewildered.

In some ways, I told Paula, it's healthy to be pulled out of the fantasy, to be reminded that you can live somewhere for years and still not be a local. It was a familiar feeling for me, and while I didn't like being hit, it was useful to be reminded that no matter how hard you work to create your own version of the world, the real one lies right outside the gates and sometimes crashes in. I've lived in a dozen cities and towns, and I can't say I ever felt fully part of any of them. Why should it be different here?

In some measure, that's because a part of me is wherever Paula and our daughter, Emma, are. Paula's work keeps her away much of the time, and Emma's happily living in Brooklyn. She and I used to see the same movies, listen to the same music, watch the same baseball games, read the same papers, and now we share few of those things.

This is as it should be when your child becomes an adult, but it hurts, still. Emma tries, but doesn't really care about cows, sheep, or barns. Nor does the latest indie movie grab me much anymore; I'm usually dead to the world by nine p.m.

My family is rarely in the same place doing the same thing anymore, and that sometimes leaves me sad, even lonely.

But it's also important and meaningful to finally know who you are, and who you aren't.

I am the proprietor of Bedlam Farm, but a citizen of nowhere.

I live on a farm, but I'm not a true farmer. Some locals call me "the dog guy," some "the sheep guy." People in town sometimes think I must be rich, not to mention crazy, for my obsession with restoring the old farmhouse and barns. "Why don't you just move into a new split-level?" one of my neighbors asked me. "You wouldn't have to do all this fixing up." I will always be seen as an oddity, a Flatlander curiosity.

But visiting New York City on a recent business trip—a place I used to work and was constantly in and out of—I found myself gawking at the Times Square lights like a tourist. A friend accompanying me laughed. "You look overwhelmed," he said. I was.

To see me going through my busy days, you wouldn't see a nowhere man. I rarely feel more comfortable than when I'm immersed in the farm's daily obligations, the grounding and comforting rituals of chores and animal care.

It's odd to think of chores that way. For most of my life,

chores—cleaning my room, mowing the lawn, doing dishes—
were something I avoided. I hated having to remember them
and being nagged about them, and I procrastinated doing
them.

Now chores define me, bind the disparate elements of my
life, keep me anchored.

Very anchored. Even when close friends or family members
come upstate, they struggle to understand how bound one is to
a place like this, how difficult it is to just pick up and leave.

Emma, the baseball fanatic, sometimes gets irritated with
me because I don't drive down to a Yankees game. She's also
suggested that on one of her visits we pop over to the Hall of
Fame in Cooperstown, about three hours away.

"I'll share the driving. It's just a few hours," she always says.
What I'm thinking is: How can I leave the farm for that long?
I'd have to make arrangements in advance; someone would
have to be on the scene much of the day, and again to tuck
everyone in at night. When you have a farm, you give up on the
idea of spontaneously taking a drive for the day.

Not that I don't have help. The Farm Goddess is here each
weekday to help haul hay, tend to the animals, keep up the
grounds and gardens. She works hard. Still, there's more to do,
many days, than I can comprehend.

I get up at five or six in the morning. At least two or three
times a week, especially in the summer, one or another dog
has ingested something vile. So the day often begins with a
mop-up.

In the winter, I usually take the dogs out only briefly—a
longer walk waits till after the animals are fed. Rose and I go
out to put a couple of bales of hay into the feeder for the sheep
and donkeys, make sure the water tubs are full, scoop out any
debris.

Next, some cat food for Mother, the barn cat, who's always waiting for me. And cookies for the donkeys, who are also waiting, braying softly. And an apple for Elvis. And a few scoops of feed for the chickens. I can no longer consider living here without Annie's help—and still, I walk miles a day from house to barns and back.

In winter, grunting, I move logs from porch to firewood holder to stoves and get the fires going. After all the animals are fed, I feed myself.

Rose and Izzy each get separate morning herding lessons. Rose desperately needs to work every day, and the herding training has been profoundly helpful for Izzy, preparing the foundations for a great training relationship. Day by day, it calms him, gives him exercise and work and focus, bonds him to me and gives him growing confidence and a sense of success. It's important.

After they're walked and fed and trained, I let most of the dogs into the yard. Pearl, survivor of many surgeries, is more of a house dog. She loves our walks, but her legs can't take too much playing or pounding, so most of the time she snores on the floor next to me while I work. Increasingly, Izzy, too, crawls under the desk and keeps me company as I write. Rose and Clem would live outside if they could. The colder and wetter the weather, the happier they are to be sitting out on the lawn. Only summer heat seems to get to them.

Having four dogs is like running a small circus—and sometimes, when Anthony is working on the farm, his black Lab Mo is also apt to be hanging around. So I move dogs around, one or two in the front yard, one or two in the back dog run, Pearl in with me.

A few times a day, we all go for quiet strolls in the woods, followed by ball-chasing sessions. And Rose and I go out into the pasture. The animals need to be moved around constantly. If it rains, they must have access to the pole barn for shelter. In warm weather, I try rotational grazing—a few weeks in one pasture, a few weeks in another, while the chewed-down grass recovers. To help preserve the pastures, I may take the sheep over the hill or across the road for an hour or two a day, to fill their bellies.

As imposing as he is, Elvis doesn't fight for his food the way sheep will. If the donkeys steal his hay, he broods and backs away. And they do steal his hay, so I keep them in different pastures.

Moving sheep is easy, for Rose. Moving donkeys isn't. They have a will of their own, won't be herded, and are wary of confinement, since they know it's often followed by the unwelcome attention of vets or farriers. So donkeys require patience. You hold up carrots, open a gate, walk through it and wait. They're often done in by their curiosity and love of snacks, so if you stand there long enough with a cookie or a carrot, they will drift slowly through the gate. Then you have to slowly move around them and close the gate. But they have to think the move is their idea, not yours. Sometimes they dart in and out a few times, just to show they can.

There's more. Bird feeders need to be replenished in winter, dogs groomed, donkeys brushed. All the animals need medical care. It's a rare week that the large-animal vet isn't here for one of my farm animals, or I'm not at the clinic with a dog, for X-rays, checkups, vaccinations, or emergencies.

And there is continuous driving. The Bedlam's Corner Variety Store, a funky old town gathering spot, carries some groceries and sundries, beer and cigarettes, and the *Glens Falls Post-Star,* but everything else requires a long trek, to Greenwich or Granville for groceries, Manchester or Rutland for specialist doctors, Saratoga for a movie. Any decent restaurant is half an hour away.

The same animal chores get repeated at dusk, sheep and donkeys and cows moved to the appropriate pastures, gotten under shelter or behind electric fences. I check water and feed and hay again, plus gates and fences. In winter, I make sure lamps and deicers are on and functioning.

The dogs eat in the late afternoon, then get a final walk. If it's cold, more firewood has to be toted in for the stoves. If not, I'm done.

And generally exhausted. Yet the truth is, I love my farm chores. I don't romanticize them; they are often draining and uncomfortable, especially in cold or rain. If I sit in a comfortable chair at any point after three p.m., I'm prone to dozing off.

I have blisters, splinters, and aching legs, knees, or arms just about all the time, in addition to my painful back. Even with more help than many farmers, I've come to understand viscerally why so many pack it in in their fifties and head for Florida to sit in a simple trailer and fish.

Still, these chores make the farm real, and make it mine. They give me intimate knowledge of the land, buildings, and animals. They settle me, the way herding grounds border collies. A restless man, I've acquired a structure to my life that's regular and—when you know the fences are tight, the animals fed, and the tanks filled with water—satisfying.

If I'm this busy and dirty and tired, I sometimes ask myself, How can I still be a Flatlander?

Belonging is largely internal, I've come to see, not only a decision by the outside world. I belong if I feel at home, if I'm comfortable with myself and what I'm doing. It's not for angry men in trucks, people in town, or other farmers to decide if I'm an outsider or not; it's a matter for me. Every day, hauling hay and herding sheep and walking dogs, I feel less an interloper, more an organic part of this place.

Still, it's always nice to get a little validation. It's rare, but when it happens, I feel closer to becoming a Citizen of Somewhere, even if I never quite get there.

HAROLD McEACHRON HAS A REPUTATION AS A TOUGH, PROGRESSIVE, prosperous farmer. At one time he had crops, cows, and, rumor has it, almost fifty thousand chickens. Now in his nineties, he still owns a lot of land, likes to be driven around in his red pickup with his venerable dog George to inspect it, and is one of the most respected farmers for miles. The father of my friend Meg Southerland, he and I became pals, taking drives around the country, going to lunch at Friendly's, his favorite restaurant, and annually visiting the Washington County Fair, where Harold, wielding his walker, makes straight for the cow-judging competitions.

He never joined the Grange or other farming groups, Harold told me, because he "doesn't like to talk all that much." On our rides, though, he does talk about the old farms and their families. He can tell me what every building we see was used for.

We could not possibly be more different. Farming runs deep in Harold's blood and lineage. His view of animals is tough and uncompromising. (George, a beloved companion of many years, has never been inside Harold's house; he sleeps in the garage, and is fed a bucket of leftovers once a day.) He wouldn't distribute cookies or treats to his animals, nor would he even keep animals that weren't headed for market.

It's often a sad journey when Harold McEachron rides past Washington County's great old farms. Most of the farmers he knew are dead or gone, their barns rotting and silos abandoned. He's outlived a culture, and watches its remnants fade every day. Farming, the center of life here when Harold was engaged in it, is now on the periphery. Those farms that escape decay or disrepair are often in the hands of Flatlanders like me, if they survive at all.

Perhaps that's why, every now and then, Harold comes to see Bedlam Farm and check on my progress. When Anthony showed him the barn restoration and told him I wanted to build an office in the middle of it, so I could work surrounded by hay, sheep and donkeys, Harold shook his head. "Heh heh." A chuckle was his only response.

He's puzzled as to why anybody would own donkeys ("hay burners") at all. But he is much impressed by my fences. "Those are darn good fences," he says approvingly. "Darn good."

One day, leaving with his grandson, he turned to me and shook my hand. "Jon, you are doing good and having fun," he said. A tribute.

I also cherished, in April, a visit from Fred DePaul, one of Vermont's best-known sheep shearers. It had taken me two years to lure him to my farm, and it was worth the wait. A genial man who loves sheep, is skilled with clippers, and loves to tell stories, he zipped through my flock in three or four hours, the two of us yakking nonstop. He told me his stories, and I told him mine.

Fred is older than me, but craggy and handsome, with a full head of grayish hair and the strength and stamina to flip hefty sheep around as if they were stuffed animals.

I was pleased to meet a craftsman who did what he loved and did it so well.

As he left on a blustery day, after several hours of wrangling and shearing, he also shook my hand. "I've really enjoyed talking with you, Jon. I respect what you've done here. This is a good farm. Your sheep are in great shape. You've found your piece of earth, haven't you?"

I was amazed by this praise, and as proud as if I'd won a Nobel prize. Prouder, maybe.

Compliments are not easy to come by here; locals are not in the habit of brightening one another's day with chirpy, upbeat commentary. Farmers' and workers' own lives are so precarious and challenging that they can't imagine why someone in my comparatively privileged position would worry about my place in their world. So when these words and good thoughts come, they mean a lot.

Walking the dogs after shearing was done, gazing at my denuded sheep and at the misty hills of Vermont just beginning to green, I thought: What if it's true? What if I've come home, for good?

I am having fun and doing some good. Maybe I've found my piece of earth.

Jon and Pearl

ELEVEN
_____

Perfect Pearl

PEARL AND I FIRST SAW ADELAIDE AT A PHYSICAL THERAPY CENTER in Manchester, Vermont. She was sitting in a wheelchair, struggling to stand and move to a table.

She looked determined, her face a mask of courage and struggle. There was also a twinkle, a kind of gallows humor. "What's next?" she asked the therapist. "Push-ups?"

Yet her drawn face and clenched teeth suggested the toll her good cheer was taking. Here, clearly, was a person in pain, but one unwilling to whine, complain, or quit.

"I'll just jog on over," she said, when her therapist asked her to move to the other side of the room.

Pearl spotted her, too, and made a tail-wagging beeline for the wheelchair in which Adelaide was seated—not, she pointed out quickly, because she needed one but because it was useful when doing leg exercises.

"Oh, my goodness, what a beautiful creature you are," said Adelaide to Pearl, who'd rested her chin on her lap. "What a love. You're here to help me get up, aren't you? You are an angel."

Pearl stared directly into her eyes as the elderly woman got to her feet, transferred to the adjacent cot, and began the somewhat arduous process of lying down.

A therapist hovered nearby, and so did Pearl, waiting patiently, giving Adelaide's hand a lick, batting her big brown eyes. Like a quiet cheerleader, she was egging her new friend on. She sat beside Adelaide for more than twenty minutes, and the therapist, initially nonplussed, was delighted; Pearl's presence seemed to energize Adelaide.

I was going to physical therapy to help heal my back. A ruptured disk was pressing painfully on a nerve because of my narrowed spinal canal. I'd received a steroid injection from a specialist in New York, which helped. Now I was hoping that with therapy, I might stave off the surgery that had seemed imminent a few months earlier.

I'd started bringing Pearl and Clementine because the therapists, dog lovers all, wanted to meet some of mine. Initially, I just brought each one in on a leash, planning to take her back to the car after a few minutes' cooing.

But Pearl created a different role for herself.

The center—one long, modern room—was filled with people of all ages recovering from a sobering variety of accidents, operations, and health problems. High school athletes, middle-aged weekend jocks, the elderly, all were working hard—to move, to heal, to rebuild and retrain muscles and joints, to ease their pain. Someone was always pumping away at an Exercycle, sitting on a big inflated ball, walking awkwardly on a balance platform.

Pearl, who behaved as if she'd seen the place a million times before, began working the room, visiting a sixteen-year-old with a torn ligament who was struggling on a cycle, then a man injured in a biking accident and an older woman recovering from a broken hip.

Vermont is an informal place in many ways; it often seems less bound by the rules, regulations, insurance, and liability concerns that so affect life elsewhere. People try to hold on to the informality and community that once characterized much of American life. In all the times Pearl came with me to the clinic, no one ever objected.

Just the opposite: When the staff saw how calm Pearl was and how warmly people responded to her, she was instantly welcome. You could tell where Pearl was by the sudden smiles, the oohs and aahs of appreciation.

In the few cases where a patient was in too much pain or just not interested in having a dog around, Pearl simply moved on. She seemed to know instinctively where she was wanted and needed, and where she wasn't.

After a few weeks, when we came into the building, I'd hear delighted greetings. "Pearl's here!" "Hey, Pearl!" "Yo, Pearl!" She made friends quickly.

I kept bringing her because the staff and patients demanded it. When I called to make an appointment, whoever answered the phone would ask, "Pearl is coming, right?" Woe to me if I showed up without her.

She was especially drawn to Adelaide. "How am I doing, Pearl?" Adelaide began asking as we saw her more regularly. Pearl always wagged her tail in approval.

Adelaide was in her early eighties, quite beautiful but terribly thin, her weathered face framed by thick, snowy hair. She was working on a series of painful exercises for a severe and intensifying case of arthritis. She could walk, but slowly, with evident discomfort. She smiled in greeting at other patients, but it was hard to watch as she struggled, sometimes using a walker, to get from one place to another. Any sort of movement appeared difficult. I assumed she was living in some sort of senior housing, perhaps an assisted-living facility.

She couldn't take her eyes off Pearl; Pearl, attention junkie that she was, usually had her head in Adelaide's lap within minutes. "I so miss having a dog," she told me softly. "But I had to let Abby go. I couldn't walk her, and our road is too busy to let a dog outside by herself. My cousin in New Hampshire took her."

I had encountered this sad phenomenon before. Letting go of a dog (or cat) was a landmark in the lives of many elderly people. Despite the voluminous research showing that pets promote mental and physical health, and ease loneliness and isolation, keeping one often just becomes too difficult for someone like Adelaide. Exercising is a problem, vet care is costly, and even simple tasks like bending over to fill a food bowl can grow difficult.

So it wasn't hard to grasp why Adelaide connected with Pearl, harder to know what was going on in the mind of a dog. My guess was that Pearl responded to neediness, to the focused attention she got from someone so happy and eager to see her. She had learned to read those signals.

Everyone at the center, I soon learned, was worried about Adelaide. Her husband had died a decade earlier, and her kids had moved away. They didn't get back to Vermont very often, and Adelaide could no longer travel long distances to see her grandchildren. Most of her friends had died or entered nursing homes.

But Adelaide, the therapists told me, wouldn't hear of leaving her house in West Pawlet, though her doctors and family had urged her to move out. Nobody liked the fact that, though almost immobile, she was living alone in an old farmhouse.

"I've been in that house for more than half a century," she told me, a steely glint materializing in her lovely blue eyes. "I expect to die there." I didn't doubt it.

Then she smiled ruefully. "I just wish I liked soap operas more, or those awful cable news channels. Life would be easier."

Life should have been easier. Unable to drive, she had to hire a teenaged neighbor to ferry her to her therapy appointments. She could no longer even manage to walk down her long driveway to get the newspaper and the mail.

Neighbors came by to help, but by and large, she said uncomplainingly, "I am on my own, and I don't want to be a bother to people." A social worker from Bennington came every couple of weeks, and so did a visiting nurse. A cousin drove in from Rutland to mow the lawn once in a while and make small repairs. She paid a neighbor ten dollars a week to go shopping for her, but she cooked for herself.

The problem was, Adelaide had come up against the American systems of health care and elder care. If she'd been an abandoned dog like Izzy, I knew, tons of people would be delighted to drive her around, find her a better place to live, ferry her to doctors' appointments, check up on her, take care of her.

But Adelaide was a retired schoolteacher, and her husband had worked for Bennington County. She said the heat treatments and exercise work she did at the clinic helped. Having a place to go also seemed to perk her up. But her insurance only provided for ten visits, and she was already on her third or fourth when we met.

After three decades of public service, it seemed strange to me that she couldn't get as much physical therapy as she needed.

Sometimes, she received letters or visits from former students, and they meant a lot to her. She brought a few to the clinic to share with me, the therapists, and Pearl.

Pearl, I saw, was increasingly important to her. Initially, we all thought the relationship cute, but it had become something more. The dog seemed to give Adelaide a bit of extra strength for her exercises, something to look forward to, a source of support. "Pearl is my vitamin," she said.

As dog lovers, we had a lot to talk about. I gave her books about dogs and she read them, scribbling notes on yellow pads when there was something she wanted to discuss. We made plans for her to visit the farm when it was warmer, so she could see the donkeys and watch Rose herd sheep.

Meanwhile, she loved having Pearl alongside her. She looked the dog in the eye, told her how beautiful she was, brought her treats. She seemed to feel that because of Pearl's many surgeries there was some understanding, a connection, between the two of them. "I think Pearl senses pain," she sometimes said. I wondered if that could be true.

What I remember most about the time they spent together was seeing them cuddled together on the floor. It was no simple matter. After her exercises, Adelaide moved from her wheelchair—using the arms as grips, as she'd been taught—and lowered herself slowly to the carpeting. Pearl curled up next to her and for twenty minutes, the two sat intertwined, Adelaide stroking Pearl's head or chest. Pearl remained absolutely still, except for an occasional lick to Adelaide's chin.

The vigilant therapists always backed away during those times. Everyone in the room saw that something unusual was happening; sometimes, the place simply quieted. These two friends were transported to their own space, and the rest of us disappeared.

When it was time to go (the therapists thoughtfully began to include snuggling-with-Pearl in Adelaide's schedule) Adelaide would—sometimes with help—struggle to her feet, put her jacket on, wave to Pearl, and go outside for her ride home. "See you next week, Pearl," she would call as she went out the door. "God willing."

Adelaide's therapist said she never saw Adelaide as animated as when Pearl was nearby, that only Pearl could have drawn her down onto the floor.

"It's as if she wants to get better for the dog," he said. "Or maybe she knows she isn't going to get too much better, but she draws strength from Pearl."

She was a great-hearted breeding and show dog, a many-ribboned champion. I'd badgered her breeder, Pam, for a couple of years to get Pearl, and the only reason I finally succeeded was because she'd been injured and Pam no longer wanted to put her through the physical stress of breeding.

Much of Pearl's life had been spent in vets' offices and surgeries, then recovering in crates. She had plentiful hardware—titanium screws holding her joints together, nylon filaments replacing ligaments—in her rear legs. She was probably often in some pain herself.

Yet Pearl retained the confidence and bearing of a champion. She took no guff from the other dogs, elbowed aside competitors for attention. Otherwise, she didn't have a menacing bone in her body, and all the other animals sensed that and were at ease around her.

She often came along sheepherding, happy to sit with me and watch Rose run around. She had no inclination to do likewise, which was a good thing. Pearl could chase a ball for a few minutes, and swimming was part of her therapy and something she loved, but most of the day she had to take it easy. Too much tearing around could cause trouble. As it was, she was likely to develop arthritis and other orthopedic problems that might shorten her life.

Already, she was so accustomed to medical interventions that whenever she went to the vet's office, even for a routine checkup, Pearl headed straight for the surgical suite. The vets and techs always greeted her by the name they'd bestowed, "Perfect Pearl."

"She is the sweetest dog in the world," one of the techs told me. "No matter what you do to her, you get a lick and a snuggle. She's never caused a single problem."

Not for me, either. Pearl has special privileges at Bedlam Farm. She's the only dog who can remain outside the fence if she wishes, because I know she won't chase anything or wander off. She can come along herding if she wants, sit out in the pasture, or visit the cows.

Indoors, I never have to crate her. Pearl doesn't raid the garbage, steal food, or chew anything not meant for her to chew (with the exception of a coyote skull, a gift from my daughter, which Pearl mistook for a bone and mashed to bits).

She is Perfect Pearl, accompanying Rose and me on our farm rounds, greeting the donkeys with sniffs and wags, licking baby Jesus, genially accepting the presence of the barn cat, Mother.

When I work, she dozes nearby on the living room rug, or in winter by the woodstove (the vet suggests the metal in her legs may get cold).

Every now and then, if I'm reading or watching TV, Pearl wanders over to rest her great head on my knee and stare at me with those brown eyes. I slip down to the floor, like Adelaide, for a hug, cuddle, and scratch.

More than anything else, she has helped me to heal: from my back troubles and pain, from the loss of Orson, from the oc-

casional loneliness I feel at the farm when Paula or Emma
aren't there, from the ups and downs of life. Pearl's a steady presence, loving and accepting, while the creatures around her—
including me—yo-yo.

Few people can look at Pearl without smiling and feeling
lifted up in some way, as Adelaide learned. Pearl was the em-
bodiment of the ethos I wanted and worked so hard to create
here: love, acceptance, peacefulness. I wanted the place and its
inhabitants to bring people pleasure, to make visitors feel welcome and accepted.

And Pearl accepts all living things. While Rose or Izzy chase
the sheep, Pearl often sits among them, tolerant of their group
mentality and slow-moving ways. While the border collies have
gone a few rounds with Mother, Pearl is always glad to see her.
The donkeys get edgy around the dogs, especially the herders,
but they sniff and nuzzle Miss Pearl, and cows have no fear of
her. She's a bit cowlike herself.

She has her limitations, of course. Pearl isn't very versatile.
She can't move fast or run quickly; she probably wouldn't be
much of a help to a hunter, and she would make a poor agility
dog. Willing but slow to respond to commands, she wouldn't
shine in the obedience ring, either. She can't even get up onto
a car seat without being lifted.

I don't really believe there's much going on behind those
enchanting brown eyes, either.

But that elemental simplicity is what makes her great. She
loves just as hard as Rose herds sheep, which may look less impressive, but perhaps does more good.

WHEN HER THERAPY VISITS WERE USED UP, ADELAIDE SAID GOOD-BYE
to everyone at the clinic, insisting that she would be fine. She

would miss seeing Pearl, she said, but she seemed resigned. It was too much for me, though.

I asked Adelaide for her address—we drove right by her house on our way into Manchester, it turned out—and asked if Pearl and I could visit when I came to my own therapy visits.

"That would be so wonderful," she said softly. I imagine she didn't really expect us to show up. Like so many people her age, she was obsessed with not being a "bother" or an "obligation" when, in truth, knowing her was a joy.

But the next week, armed with cookies, books, and a fruit basket, we turned into the driveway of her small farmhouse.

My own farm was teeming with animals, activity, life. This house almost looked abandoned.

They say in the country that you can tell from looking at a house if the man who lived in it has died. It sounds strange, and sexist, to outsiders, but there's some truth to it. Upstate, it is most often men who ride mowers, paint clapboard and trim, rake up leaves and fallen twigs. Adelaide's house looked neglected; the man of the house was long dead.

The gutters had rotted and water stains dotted the roofline. Paint had peeled from the porch. The yards and gardens were weed-choked, filled with fallen leaves and broken tree limbs. Adelaide desperately needed Anthony for a few months.

I knocked and heard her calling that we should come in. The house was tidier inside than out, furnished with old upholstered chairs and mahogany tables. The interior smelled musty, the wallpaper had faded, but the place was relatively neat and clean.

We found Adelaide sitting on the living room sofa, and Pearl wasted no time in rushing over, laboriously climbing up and curling up next to her friend. Adelaide apologized for her housecoat and slippers. She also apologized for not having made tea or a pie. Pearl didn't mind. In a minute, her head was in Adelaide's lap, and she was snoring.

THE ROOM WAS ARRANGED SO THAT ALMOST EVERYTHING WAS within reach of Adelaide on the couch.

She had a new seventeen-inch TV and a new cable dish, courtesy of her kids, but she rarely turned the thing on. "Yuck," she said. "I'd rather read or sew." She listened most of the day to an old radio.

When her neighbors came by, they set her up with tea and books; the rest of the day, she was on her own.

"I miss small things, like swimming in the pond down the road," she said. "I miss cooking and walking through the woods. And, of course, Abby." A photograph on the mantel showed a younger Adelaide with a sleek black Lab. She noticed my noticing. "This is great country for a Lab," she said. "Ponds and woods everywhere. So much trouble to get into—skunks, raccoons, porcupines." Yes, I nodded, I knew this only too well.

We chatted for a few minutes, and then I helped out in the kitchen a little. It was spare, with a toaster and microwave. The freezer was stocked with frozen dinners; there was a loaf of whole wheat bread and a carton of milk in the fridge, some pears and apples in a bowl on the counter. The general store sometimes delivered soup and sandwiches at lunchtime, if the proprietor wasn't too busy. I got the feeling that, sometimes, Adelaide skipped meals.

I also saw the rows of medicines and vitamins, liquids and pills, and wondered how she possibly kept them all straight. She never talked about her health, but I knew from the therapist at the center that it was worsening.

So I kept our visit brief, not wanting to tire her. Pearl got off the couch as quietly as she got on.

IT WAS ODD ABOUT PEARL. MOST OF THE TIME, SHE SEEMED SO SIM-ple, not a complicated creature. But once in a while, as with Ade-laide, she had a gift for tapping into the complexity of situations.

At the therapy center, Pearl always seemed to read the place perfectly, avoiding people who didn't want to see her, heading straight for those who did. She never jumped on anyone, pushed too hard, or pestered. "She's always appropriate," mar-veled one of the other patients, another of Pearl's buddies.

When it was time for people to lie down with a heat pad, Pearl simply let them be. When they needed encouragement to pedal harder on the bike, or a pat on her head seemed to make them hurt less, she would materialize.

I'd never trained Pearl for this kind of work. She was not a therapy dog, at least not officially. But almost any dog can be a therapy dog in a way, given the right genetics, the right circum-stances and opportunity. Pearl came by it naturally, without an identifying vest or bandanna.

My own therapy proved relatively successful. My back pain eased, my mobility improved. I began to fantasize that I might not need surgery.

And Pearl and I kept visiting Adelaide. As I figured out what she liked—she never asked for anything—we began to bring things: sandwiches, salads, flowers, magazines, pictures of Pearl and the other dogs and animals on the farm. Ade-laide always offered to pay, told me the food wasn't necessary, complained that we were going out of our way, doing too much. The food, I noticed, was always gone the next time we came. But I didn't offer to help with personal tasks like cleaning or washing dishes; I don't think she would have liked or allowed it.

A cousin drove her out to my farm one balmy afternoon in late winter, and she sat in his car while Rose escorted the sheep down the driveway. Adelaide was failing, it seemed to me. She didn't have the energy to come out and give the donkeys the carrots she'd brought, so I fed them while she watched from the car. Then I helped Pearl climb into the backseat so the two could have a cuddle. Adelaide loved seeing the farm, but twenty minutes was enough.

Still, we'd got very comfortable with each other other. I looked forward to our talks, in which there was no pressure on either of us to be scintillating, impressive, witty. We mused about how the country had changed, how kids were different, how politics had grown so ugly, how people still killed one another in faraway wars, how small-town life in places like Vermont was vanishing.

Adelaide came from another time. She found much of contemporary culture, technology, and politics beyond comprehension. She'd never used a computer or a cell phone. Her life was quiet, almost beautifully so, even under these diminished circumstances, her home a soothing, restful place. Visiting her there didn't seem anything like a chore or an obligation; it was a pleasure.

Not long after stopping therapy, Adelaide had to move into a downstairs bedroom; she couldn't manage the steps any longer, not twice a day.

But she and Pearl continued their usual routine: Pearl trotted into the house, crawled onto the sofa, curled up alongside her. Sometimes I left Pearl with her while I went to my therapy appointment, then picked her up on the way back. She was invariably in the same spot she'd been in when I left.

Adelaide never complained about her illness or pain, and I

didn't ask much. She just said things would take their course, and you could see that they were.

IN APRIL, THERE WAS NOBODY HOME AT ADELAIDE'S WHEN I CAME BY with Pearl. A neighbor told me she'd been taken to Bennington Hospital. When I called the next night, the woman who answered told me she was Adelaide's daughter. Her mother, she said, would be home from the hospital the following day. She'd heard all about Pearl from her mother, she said, and wanted to meet her. And her mother seemed desperate to see Pearl.

Did she use that word, I asked—desperate?

"Yes," she said.

A couple of days later, I called to see if we could stop by. Yes, if we could come quickly, Adelaide's daughter said; her mother was being transferred to a nursing facility. Pearl and I jumped into the car.

We got to West Pawlet quickly, but a private ambulance was already waiting outside. When we went inside, Adelaide was lying on a wheeled gurney in the living room. She waved and winked. Pearl, looking puzzled, came over and rested her head on Adelaide's shoulder.

Adelaide said nothing; perhaps she could no longer speak. I squeezed her hand, and she was rolled out to the ambulance. I didn't know what to say; anything I thought of seemed unnecessary or obvious.

Pearl followed, tail wagging. I thought for a second that she might jump into the ambulance, but that would have been decidedly un-Pearl. She was not impulsive or unpredictable.

"Let's go, girl," I said, and she trotted over to my car, waiting for me to lift her in.

Pearl and I continue to go to physical therapy, usually once a week, sometimes twice. There, gradually, I learned more about how much pain Adelaide had been in, how serious her health problems were, how much of a struggle it must have been to talk with and entertain us, how much Pearl must have meant to her.

Pearl has moved on, of course, in the delightfully adaptable way dogs do. Some like to think of dogs as eternally loyal, pining always for the people they love.

I don't see it that way. They love us unconditionally, but, when necessary, they move on and love someone else. It's their great gift, something that shouldn't be denied or misunderstood. Pearl loved her breeder dearly for years, and now she loves me just as much. In between, she will take on special cases like Adelaide.

So Pearl has made new friends at the therapy center. Her relationships aren't as close as with Adelaide, but she's spending a lot of time with Samantha, a sixteen-year-old track star recovering from breaking her kneecap in a fall. Samantha has recently asked to schedule her appointments to coincide with mine. The receptionist sometimes jokes that I'll never be able to stop physical therapy, because too many people need Pearl. As it happens, I think she has little to worry about.

I miss that brave, gentle woman struggling so hard to spend the end of her life in dignity.

Perhaps Pearl misses her, too, I think. She always looks into the bay where Adelaide got her treatment. But Samantha has taken to bringing liver treats.

Dogs are fortunate, I think, to have less consciousness and self-awareness than we do. Pearl loves totally and ceaselessly, and especially connects to those who need and want her nurturing.

How nice, I often think, that she will never really know what she did for Adelaide, or understand why her friend is gone. She will simply turn those big brown eyes elsewhere, and bring light into other darkened corners.

TWELVE

Anger Management

THE TRAINING PEN IS A FENCED SQUARE IN THE MIDDLE OF THE PAS-
ture where I can put the sheep, so that dogs learn to work with
them without getting too close. I was out there the other
morning, trying to teach Izzy the directional commands—
"come bye" and "away to me"—that enable a border collie to
herd, rather than simply chase.

He wasn't getting them. He seemed excited for some reason, disconnected from me, pursuing his agenda rather than
mine.

There may be more difficult training tasks in the canine
world, but there's no doubt that successfully working border
collies with sheep requires prodigious amounts of patience, experience, and composure. It's a frantic, confusing, fast-moving,
occasionally risky process. Dogs can tear ligaments, slice paws,

break legs, get trampled. Sheep can get bitten, bang into posts and fences, even suffer heatstroke.

In our desire to love and humanize dogs, we often forget their carnivorous natures and wild instincts. Seeing a border collie's arousal when it's introduced to sheep will cure that.

Otherwise sweet-tempered, calm pets can turn into rapacious little wolves, too frenzied to hear or pay attention to the humans speaking or (often) yelling at them; they often go into a kind of trance, beyond our control.

We know what we want them to do, but we're reminded that what's most natural for them—running down the sheep and devouring them—is not what Animal Planet celebrates.

It takes a truly daunting amount of repetitive work to get them to understand that the point isn't to chase the sheep, but to move them calmly and professionally from one place to another without injuries to sheep, dogs, or people.

Many elements go into training border collies—voice commands, movement, hand signals or whistles—but a basic requirement is being able to get your dog to move left and right, stay or slow down, stop, lie down. Few of them want to behave that way in the presence of sheep. Izzy wasn't showing much inclination to that morning.

In fact, the most enduring memories I have of working with sheep and dogs is the unsavory spectacle of so many people— myself included—screaming at their dogs.

I tend to forget sometimes how attached my dogs are to me, how much attention they pay to my moods. Herding reminds me, dramatically.

Rose is not an overly sensitive being, not after years of living and working with me. She's confident, experienced; she knows what to do. Yet I yell at her all the time: "Rosie, let's go! Get moving! Bring those sheep down here! Look back— there's two left behind!" As much as I love, admire, and appreciate my astounding dog, it's a rare day I don't bellow one command or another. Mostly, she does her job and ignores my histrionics.

But Izzy, still so new, is growing hardwired into my moods. If I look at him crosswise or raise my voice, he freezes, cowers, or backs up. He's not a dog you can yell at, not after only a few months. Though he's not an abused or traumatized dog, neither has he yet achieved the experience to push a flock around. He does, however, show astonishing potential.

He loves working with Rose, in part because he can take cues from her, studying her moves. But that's not sufficient. If I want to train him well, to herd sheep or do anything else, I have to be positive and enthusiastic, patient and clear, day after day, month after month. This is a dog that can easily be damaged, have his confidence eroded and spirit broken.

Sadly, qualities like having patience, taking a long view, aren't natural traits for me. In fact, they're lifelong challenges.

When a dog like Izzy lands in your life, however, you have a responsibility to do right by him. That means more changes for me, another chance to improve my wretched self, even into my sixth decade.

It's a significant challenge for a man who carries much anger, buried in my consciousness like radioactive waste, yet not far enough from the surface. I'm angry at my parents for the difficult childhood my sister and I had to endure, at other family members for ignoring our plight. I'm ticked off, like so many people, at a world plagued by cruelty and violence, obsessed with bigness and profit, increasingly uninterested in loyalty and integrity.

Lots of things make my temper flare: the battered rescue dogs left in my barn; men who would rather fight than talk; the way elderly friends live in dread of the health care system. I admire more Eastern practices of acceptance, but I suspect I can't achieve that in this life.

But what the dogs and the farm and its animals have given me is the opportunity to be less angry, more patient and loving; to grasp concepts like humility and mercy, not as abstract notions to read about or spout, but as principles that creatures like Izzy force me to live every day.

I will do as well as Izzy does. He will reflect my shortcomings, mirror my growth. If I can be less angry, he will be well. Either way, there will be no hiding our progress, or lack of it: All anybody has to do is look at Izzy to peer into my soul.

I could not choose a more challenging yardstick than sheepherding with border collies. Bowling would be smarter and a lot easier.

Whatever anger lies suppressed but lurking within comes boiling to the surface, and it's so easy to mess up a dog with it. I fought hard to curb this anger with Orson, already scarred when he entered my life, and I won't ever know if my inability to fully conquer it contributed in some way to his death. I do know that I was repeatedly and demonstrably angry with him, and I'm sure he suffered for it. I am passionately resolved that Izzy won't suffer the same way.

As Izzy got increasingly agitated and visibly confused, alas, my voice began rising. Why couldn't I get his attention? Circling to the right when I said "come bye" seemed a simple command. He was a smart dog; he'd done it before. Why wasn't he getting it this morning? Why was he blowing me off?

Izzy was on the opposite side of the training pen, the sheep between us, and he was running in circles. I banged my walking stick on the pen's metal gate. He startled at the clang and jumped back. "Listen to me!" I yelled. "Come bye, *now!*"

He looked even more confused. I yelled at him to lie down, and he did.

Annie was walking past, toting water for the donkeys. "You see that?" I asked, impatiently. "What's wrong with him?"

Annie has unusual genes: Guile and anger appear missing from her psyche. She doesn't know how to be anything but honest, and her advocacy for animals can quickly turn ferocious.

"What's wrong with *you?*" was her response.

I was surprised. "What do you mean?"

"You're edgy and angry. You're yelling at him. He's picking up on your anger and it's freaking him out."

This was so obviously true that it was embarrassing to have to hear about it from someone else. Which demonstrated precisely what I believed about my own shortcomings: A voiceless dog could practically shout them to the world. If Annie could see it, so could anybody. So could I.

Izzy was losing it because I was angry. My back hurt, it was already a hot day, the flies had recently hatched and were all over me. Allergies had been keeping me up hacking at night, and construction on the big barn meant banging and hammering outside my window all day. Visitors and business trips were disrupting my work. I felt tense, disgruntled, grumpy.

So I left the pasture and sat down on the stone steps leading to the back door. Izzy loped over and crawled into my lap. I bent my head and kissed him on the nose and he wriggled further into my arms, his tail switching. I took a liver treat from my pocket and put it on his tongue.

"I'm sorry, Iz," I said, as he flopped over to get his belly rubbed. "I think we hit the jackpot with each other, but as a human, I have many more shortcomings than you. My temper, for instance. I love you to death and I'll try to do better, to be the human you deserve."

When I stood up, Izzy spun around and, in the finest border collie tradition, was ready to work again, to start over and give it another shot. We walked back to the training pen, and no insurance salesman was ever more chipper or upbeat than I.

I waited until he moved to the right, then whooped for joy—"Good come bye! Good come bye!" Transformed by praise and enthusiasm, Izzy raced to the right when I said, "Come bye." And he streaked left when I yelled (happily), "Away!"

He did it several times, in fact. Annie looked stunned. "I can't believe that's the same dog I just saw. Or the same person."

We went through our routine for another five minutes, then I pointed behind me and yelped (warmly), "Come out, Iz! Come on out." He rushed toward me and leaped up into my arms, beside himself with excitement and pleasure.

Do you see, dumbass, what the dog is teaching you? I asked myself. Is it finally beginning to work through your impenetrable skull? Anger does not work. It's not effective, not with people or with dogs. And this new dog is a messenger here to drive this truth once more into your woeful consciousness.

So I've developed a different protocol, an innovation, so far as I know, in the herding world. Border collie snobs were already annoyed with me, because I have border collies in the first place (they think people like me shouldn't), because I don't take them to competitions (too many uptight people shouting at their dogs), and because I've homeschooled them, avoiding the pros and adapting their training to life on the farm. My methods are admittedly unconventional. Rose is a true heroine, but there will be no championship ribbons in her future. The snobs won't approve of my new technique with Izzy, either.

But now when we go herding, I take Iz over to the training pen and I—not the dog—sit on the ground. He comes rushing over and jumps into my lap, and I hold and pat him as I take a dozen deep breaths and look up at the vast sky. I sit like this for five minutes, sometimes ten, as Izzy fixes his developing "eye" on the sheep. He glares and stares; the sheep stare back; and we all wait.

When I'm calm, ready, in control, we get up and go to work. I send Izzy to the sheep, and I give him his directional commands. If I see him halt, look agitated or confused, get hyper or aroused, then we leave the pasture and go back into the house. This happened three or four times a week at first, then once or twice. For the past couple of weeks, though, we haven't had to leave the field at all.

Our lessons have been successful, fun, effective. Izzy is becoming a first-class working dog right before my eyes. He knows "come bye" and "away." He's never put his mouth on a sheep. He gives great eye. The sheep no longer stampede away from him, and he no longer gives chase.

After our lessons, he lies down near the flock. I often leave him sitting there as they graze, while I go inside, check my messages, have a mug of coffee.

Each day, he's working better and more effectively with Rose. Each week, I give him more complex tasks to perform. He can now bring the sheep out from the pasture to the meadow, single-handed, then move them back in. It's miraculous for so new a dog, and for one who spent three years inside a fence.

I'LL CONFESS THAT WHILE I LOVE HERDING SHEEP WITH THE DOGS, IT'S not a purely necessary function. Marching through the woods and across meadows with the flock is deeply calming, a satisfying accomplishment, and a timeless ritual that connects me to Nature and to animals.

But do I really need to train the dogs to herd? I don't. The sheep have sufficient pasture and would just as soon not be herded, thanks. Rose lives for working with sheep, but Izzy might just as happily run alongside the ATV or take a ride into town. But herding has another function now, and it's not only the dogs that are being trained.

Though the lesson is long overdue, I'm beginning to grasp this anger thing, and work hard to conquer it in the time left to me.

Sometimes even Rose has the potential to set me off. If she gets too intense, and she's working in close quarters near gates and fences, she will once in a while drive the sheep right into me.

This really didn't matter much at first; I could handle the occasional bump or fall. But as my back troubles intensified, my need for calm and distance when herding has grown.

We had one of those episodes in late spring. We were taking the sheep across the road to graze. As the sheep charged toward the pasture and its inviting, newly sprouted grass, Rose got cranked up and galloped over to head them off. She won't let the sheep dash across the road without pausing and moving at my command; that can be dangerous.

But this day, my thoughts elsewhere, I was walking slowly ahead as sheep and dog reversed course and came plowing into me, nearly knocking me over. I began to do what I usually do: scream at Rose to get back and move slowly.

But I stopped and whistled. Rose paused at this odd behavior, eyes wide, and looked at me in confusion. What did that mean?

I blew her a kiss and spoke in a whisper, causing her to tilt her ears to pick up what I was saying. Rose, more than any other creature, is finely attuned to my moods and signals.

"Hey there, sweetheart," I said softly. "How about slowing down, giving the old man some space?"

Pause.

"Please?"

Rose sat down and stared at me curiously. The sheep waited to see what was up. I walked to the road and quietly asked Rose to bring the sheep. She complied, and the flock trotted slowly into the meadow and began to munch. Mission accomplished.

Elvis and Luna

THIRTEEN

Monster Love

ELVIS HAD SETTLED IN REMARKABLY WELL, GIVEN THAT I'D NEVER had a steer before. An intensely social creature, he reminded me a bit of the animated character Shrek: All he wanted was love and attention, yet most people wanted to flee his approach.

Which was understandable. Whenever someone opened the gate, no matter where in the pasture Elvis was, he came thundering down the slope toward his visitor.

It was a true test of nerves. When Elvis launched his nearly two thousand pounds, it wasn't easy for him to slow or stop. And the hill was steep. He'd left broad skid marks all over the pasture.

But I always brought along an apple or pear or carrot, and held it up as he came charging toward me. With my other hand extended, I yelled, "Stay!" Much of the time, he did.

Once or twice he got excited, swung his huge head, and

sent me sprawling. Then he leaned over and licked me with his enormous drooly tongue, like a two-story Newfoundland.

Cars continuously screeched to a halt on the road at the sight of him, his head extended over the fence as he took in the view of farms, pastures, cows, a couple of alpacas. He could stand for hours staring out at the world beyond.

I'd become quite attached to him. He was gentle, loving, even a bit needy. We had some astoundingly peaceful moments, I scratching his neck while he bellowed softly. Sometimes the two of us gazed out at the view together.

But Annie worried. He'd spent his whole life with a herd of milking cows, and now he was by himself. Since the donkeys wanted no part of him, and the sheep stole his hay, I kept him in his own paddock behind the big barn. Was he lonely? Several times a day, he came up to the pasture gate—now electrified like a state prison's—to draw closer to the other animals and moo mournfully. Except for the baby donkey, they would all quickly move as far away as they could get. Only Jesus would come over and check Elvis out from the opposite side of the gate.

To be honest, fond as I was of him, I didn't really want him strolling around the farm. He could walk through any fence I had, practically without noticing. If he swung his head against my hay feeder, he would almost surely demolish it.

And he also didn't really know how to play well with others. A few times I'd tried bringing the donkeys and the sheep into the paddock with him. He appeared delighted to have company, but when he galloped into their midst, the sheep fled and the donkeys hid behind trees. Elvis looked disappointed. Maybe he *was* lonely.

Apart from these social issues, though, he was thriving. He ate about two bales of hay a day, and once May came, took to nibbling on newly sprouted leaves and the plentiful grass the rainy spring had spawned.

And then, only a few weeks after he arrived, I got a call from Annie's best friend. Nicole and her husband owned a beautiful farm just outside the village. She and Annie shared a passionate love for animals, and Nicki's small herd of cows and horses were fed the best hay and grain, sheltered in warm and spotless barns, given the freshest green pasture. They all had names, not numbers.

Now Nicki's husband was being promoted and transferred, and they had to move. Amid the chaos and tears, Nicki was frantic to find good homes for her animals—in particular, her favorite cow, Luna, a brown-and-white three-year-old.

Nicki didn't want Luna to go to a dairy farm. She wanted her to live somewhere she could graze freely and continue to get special grain treats, and where some idiot would feed her forever. Naturally, I agreed.

I called Paula, who by now was so bewildered by the parade of creatures through what she'd started calling Jon Katz's Wild Kingdom that she just mumbled something about the cost of hay and barely argued.

I called my friend Pete, the dairy farmer who'd sold me Elvis, and asked if he could transport Luna in his livestock trailer. One wrinkle was that Nicki would not allow Luna to be coerced; she couldn't be prodded, kicked, or clobbered into the trailer. (Pete's response: "What?") Instead, Nicki wanted the trailer brought to her farm where, over several days, Luna would be offered hay and grain inside. Then, when she walked in of her own accord, Nicki would close the trailer gate and Luna soon would be on her way to Bedlam Farm.

This was clearly not the way Pete traditionally lured cows onto a trailer, but he understood that he was dealing with a different philosophy and genially agreed. So one Monday he, his brother Dean, and Annie drove over to Nicki's to drop off the trailer and see whether Luna (a slip of a lass at nine hundred pounds) would climb aboard. As it happened, when Nicki brought out a tub of grain, Luna hopped onto the trailer without two seconds' hesitation. Nicki said a tearful good-bye, and the entire entourage drove to my place.

A delicious collision of cultures ensued at my pasture gate when the trailer backed in. Dean and Peter Hanks, dairymen for decades, were there in their Big Green Farms shirts. Annie and Nicki, animal lovers from another realm, were standing by with grain and apples, to make sure Luna was not pressured, coerced, or distressed by the move.

Paula, still wary of the monster living in her backyard, was on hand to witness this spectacle. And I, almost a bystander on my own farm, was watching with Izzy. Izzy, it turned out, was oddly calm around farm animals; he simply lay down and let them nuzzle him.

A few yards away, sitting on the front lawn, Rose was intently studying the trailer and preparing her game plan.

Elvis's head came up as soon as he saw the trailer and heard Luna's moo. He mooed back. Hers was a guttural alto bray; his was deeper. We saw him begin to dance around. A friend like me! Maybe a girlfriend! The two started talking to each other right away.

Elvis's dancing around the pasture was a sobering sight, causing all the humans to back up quickly. I went over and tapped him on the nose, saying, "Yo, dude, chill." He retreated a bit, and we swung the gate open. Luna, uncoerced, trotted off the trailer and into the pasture.

Elvis was beside himself with joy. He sniffed Luna, and licked her, then the two of them took off, frisking around the pasture. He literally kicked up his heels.

I'm not sure what a happy pair of cows ought to look like, to be honest, but these two seemed quite pleased to meet. From the first day, they became inseparable; now we rarely see one without the other close by.

At night, the two go off to sleep under an apple tree, and Luna sometimes rests her head on Elvis's monstrous back. She's no pushover, though. When Elvis started to get fresh—a truly daunting sight—Luna swung her smaller head around and conked him on the nose. He desisted.

In the morning now, when I come out, I see the two of them at the top of the hill, curled up together like kittens, taking in the view of the valley.

These days I begin my morning by hopping on the ATV with carrots and apples and seeking out the happy couple. Usually I come puttering by, Izzy or Rose running alongside. When I hold out an apple and Luna or Elvis snorts and scarfs it down, I feel like I'm reaching for the brass ring on an old merry-go-round.

At the end of the day, when I have more time, I stop, distribute more apples and carrots, and scratch Elvis behind the ear, which he loves, lowering his head to the ground. He is, I think, trying to learn to be gentle. Love does soften the heart.

It rained for five days in a row in May, and during one nasty nighttime windstorm I put on my parka and went out to check on the animals. The donkeys and sheep were in the pole barn, the chickens had roosted, but Elvis and Luna had no shelter for the summer. I took my zillion-watt torch and swept the beam along until I found a stand of trees. Elvis was lying next to one of the trees, Luna huddled just below him, using him as a windbreak, the two pressed tightly together.

Lots of people who keep animals believe they should always have at least two of a species, that the company of their own kind simply makes animals more comfortable and content. It was why I had multiple donkeys and hens; the dogs, too, seemed calmer and happier when part of a small herd.

Seeing these two lying together in the windswept rain, I decided this was one animal theory I could embrace.

Fanny, Lulu, Jeannette, Jon, and Clem

FOURTEEN

Joint Custody

THE FARM WAS MORE CHAOTIC THAN USUAL THIS SPRING, WITH THE barn under construction. Doors and gates had been removed and stashed here and there; scaffolding and tractors and piles of rubble had taken over the barnyard; the animals' feeding spots and shelter had been shifted around.

So it was not terribly surprising that someone had opened a pasture gate and then not properly replaced it. The donkeys discovered this first, most likely, and then the sheep probably followed them across the road to the inviting pasture across from the farmhouse.

Rose was frantic when we went outside that afternoon, hearing or sensing where the sheep had gone, and went dashing for the meadow. When I followed, I saw the sheep and donkeys spread out, crunching on the taller grass there. It was a lovely, peaceful scene, so I let everyone stay put and eat. Rose helped keep everybody in the center of the meadow for an hour or so, then rounded up the sheep and moved them back across the road into their own pasture. The donkeys followed without much back talk, helped along by some carrots and apples.

Almost the entire time, I heard an intermittent whimper from the yard and looked up to see Clem's soulful eyes peering from the other side of the gate. She wanted to come along.

When I think of this spring, some of the images lodged in my mind are of Clementine's gazing through windows and gates, rushing to doors, wanting to come along to places she couldn't easily go.

Those aren't the only images, of course. I can picture nights on the sofa, too. Like this one:

The Yankees were getting drubbed by the Oakland A's, and, since it was a West Coast game, I was up late, watching via my new, improved satellite dish, the only way to get decent TV reception in an area this rural. I had a bowl of peanuts in my lap and Clementine snuggled next to me, sleeping soundly. It was a chilly night, and it was nice to feel her warmth, her affection. Every now and then, I slipped a shelled peanut into her mouth and, still mostly asleep, she inhaled it with a crunch, sighed, and went back to sleep without even opening her eyes.

She and Rose were the only two of my current dogs that had come to me as puppies, and Rose was not a cuddler. But Clem was my TV-watching buddy. She loved late movies, the Yankees and *The Sopranos,* and microwaved popcorn. She sat curled alongside me through many *American Idol* dramas.

Her greatest interest, however, was in dozing. She would hop up onto the sofa, slurp my face for a moment, then lie down and conk out, awakening only to pick up stray crumbs from whatever I was snacking on and to give my hand an occasional lick.

I can picture predawn mornings in bed, too. Often Clem and I had been battling for space and blankets all night. She liked to crawl up onto my chest when Winston began his crowing, and plop down. I could barely breathe beneath her weight. She methodically licked my chin, then my nose and cheeks; then she put her head on my shoulder. I often simply put my arms around her, and the two of us had a long cuddle, then went back to sleep.

BUT THEN CAME THE THURSDAY EVENING PEARL AND I WERE headed to a talk at a local library. She was the dog I brought to public events these days. She greeted everyone enthusiastically but quietly, didn't stray from my side, and in a few minutes, would find fans to scratch her belly. After a while, I'd hear snoring. People loved her, and vice versa.

Clementine, also intensely social, was less predictable at such gatherings and required greater vigilance. She loved the attention, but she also trawled for food, might put her paws in people's laps, and was simply more energetic. Most of the time, she was quite well behaved; but now and then she grew restless.

Pearl was easier. But as I lifted her into the back of the car, I saw Clem looking out the window. She wanted to come along.

I KNEW THE MINUTE IZZY JOINED THE HOUSEHOLD THAT MY LIFE with dogs would change once more. Everyone has his own notion of an optimal life with dogs, and is entitled to it. Mine involves two or three dogs, at most. Two has always been fairly simple; three and beyond is a pack. Some people can handle all the feeding, training, walks, vet treks, vomit, and diarrhea. Some, like me, can handle it sometimes but not always.

I knew even as I allowed it to happen that four dogs would be too many. It's difficult for anyone to control four dogs on walks, or to spend enough one-on-one time with each of them.

I end up yelling too often—"Hey, no street!" or "Drop it!" or "Come, *now!*" My voice gets louder, more exasperated; walks grow tiring and a bit chaotic; training becomes sloppy, since much of the time, the dogs can't discern which of them I'm talking to.

Four dogs on a farm pose particular challenges, surrounded as they are by mud and manure, rotting wild animal carcasses, barbwire and brambles. The border collies get stickleburrs matted in their fur. The Labs eat awful stuff and vomit it right back up.

I can't count the number of nights I woke up to the sound of heaving and barfing. I've dubbed my response the Two-Minute Diarrhea Drill, but of course it takes longer. Dog lovers know this routine only too well. Everyone has his own techniques, traded at dog parks and runs and online.

My own: Hustle downstairs in the dark, grab a trash bag and some freezer bags, plus two pieces of cardboard, a spray bottle of odor remover, a roll of paper towels. I use the cardboard as a scooper to get up as much of the goop as I can and dump it in the freezer bags so it doesn't stink up the whole house, then put them in the larger trash bag. I may have to wield more cardboard. Then I pour on the odor and stain remover and sponge it up with the paper towels. The trash bag fills up with messy cardboard and plastic bags.

No matter what I do, spillage occurs. If the dog was in a crate, I remove the mats carefully (more spillage), unzip the covers, and put them in the washer. Sometimes I have to take the plastic bottom out and hose it down.

Often there's ancillary damage around the edges of the

crates. More bags, towels, odor remover. If the dog has also soiled herself or himself, it's a whole other scenario.

With four hunting and working dogs on a farm, it's become a common, even frequent scenario. The washer and dryer may be going for hours.

I am perfectly willing to do it, but of course, there are consequences. I rarely get back to sleep. I often strain my back. The following day can be tough in terms of my chores, my work, and my energy.

The only way to avoid this ungodly ritual, however, is to keep the dogs fenced all day, and what is the point of living on a farm with all these lovely acres if you're going to do that?

But as the weeks passed, I felt I had too many dogs. Four dogs at the door, jostling to be the first one out for a walk. Four dogs to keep track of and throw balls for. Four dogs eating stuff and getting sick, needing shots and Lyme prevention and antibiotics. It grew hard to find time to train them all, to give them the work they needed and deserved, and still to attend to the other things I needed to do—especially when two of the dogs were energetic young border collies and two were strong yellow Labs.

Before Izzy came, I felt I had it under control. In the weeks since, I was losing it. Dog care was growing more complicated, and other things were beginning to pile up in my life.

This was entirely my fault, a foreseeable and avoidable problem—had I only declined to go see Izzy that day on his farm.

But once I did go, I just couldn't leave him in his small fenced quarters by himself. Nor could I give him up once I brought him home to the farm.

All my dogs have been great dogs. Yet I had given one away a few years earlier. Homer, a two-year-old border collie, had come up to Bedlam Farm with Orson and Rose, but almost from the first he had trouble. Orson tortured and tormented him; the sheepherding took a toll on his legs and his stamina. We'd had many delightful hours together at my upstate cabin, and herding on a friend's farm in Pennsylvania, and strolling through my suburban town. Yet I'd never felt the bond, the strong chemistry, with Homer that I had with my other dogs. Over time, I decided that he would do best as an only dog, and he went to live with some New Jersey neighbors and friends whose son, Max, adored him.

As I monitored his transition, by phone and on visits, Homer was visibly happier and so much more relaxed in his new home that I regretted having waited so long.

It was the first time I'd recognized that a dog of mine, however well cared for, might just be better off living elsewhere; that it was not only acceptable to give a dog to someone else but, sometimes, the right thing to do, a moral act. I had pangs about Homer for some time, and Paula missed him a great deal. But my notion of dog advocacy had expanded to include the idea that even if a change isn't swell for us, it might be good for a dog. Now I wondered if such a change—though it would be even harder this time—might be good for Clementine.

I'm not one who can collect dogs and simply feed and love them. Dogs, especially border collies and Labs, are bred to do things, to work with humans, to learn and serve. Although two of mine qualified as rescue dogs, I can't acquire dogs simply because they're needy, then allow them to be contented lawn ornaments; that offends my sense of responsibility.

Yet feeding four dogs can be a challenge. Keeping track of deworming, anti-flea and anti-tick medications, and dietary supplements like glucosamine is difficult. Pearl alone needs regular doses of this and that, along with massage, swim therapy, and acupuncture for her battered legs.

Plus, there are the casualties and crises of normal canine life. Pearl got caught on barbwire down in the woods on one of our strolls, slashing one of her good legs. The vet bandaged her up and prescribed antibiotics. Rose came back from a walk smeared in deer scat she'd rolled in and needed a bath at once. As the weather finally warmed, there were pests and parasites to worry about, and confrontations with porcupines, snakes, feral cats, and raccoons.

And then there was training. It wasn't, to me, just a question of obedience, of learning "sit" or "stay," but something much deeper, more profound, part of my obligation to these remarkable animals. I often recalled one of my favorite injunctions, from the Talmud: "You are not obligated to complete the work, but neither are you free to abandon it."

Dogs, especially the proud and intense working breeds that I love to live and work with, need and deserve time, attention, training, and work, along with affection. From the minute Izzy arrived, this philosophy of mine was leading toward a crisis of conscience.

Even before his arrival, I sometimes worried that Clementine wasn't getting what she deserved. It wasn't a question of her happiness. Clem was much loved, loved back, got plenty of exercise chasing balls and going for walks, enjoyed the company of people and other dogs. She had, by almost any measure, a good life.

Yet I couldn't help but notice that, more and more, she was peering in from the periphery of our lives.

Each of the other dogs seemed to have developed special roles and functions. Pearl came to physical therapy with me, and to most of my readings and public appearances, as she was incapable of being too boisterous and could be relied on to fall asleep within minutes of my starting to talk.

I was herding with both Izzy and Rose, but I didn't bring Clem along; that would mean too many dogs to keep an eye on, along with the sheep. Whenever I passed by with the flock, though, I saw her watching pensively from the front yard; sometimes, she whined softly.

Not a hunter, I didn't really have work for Clem to do, nor time to offer her more than perfunctory play. Clem couldn't run as fast alongside the ATV as the border collies could, and I didn't want her to risk injury trying. She would have charged after balls and sticks forever, but she had to content herself with ten minutes twice a day, given the herding work that Rose needed, the therapy prescribed for Pearl, the training that Izzy urgently required, and all the other demands of the farm and of earning our livelihood.

Clem wasn't living a miserable existence, nor did she have any consciousness of her plight. But I feared I wasn't really meeting my responsibility to her.

This was a beautiful, energetic, loving, and remarkable dog. Didn't she deserve more? She was as much of a working dog as Rose, but had no work to do. Cuddling on the sofa with me at night, much as I appreciated it, wasn't quite enough.

She was being left out, not getting the training she needed, the attention she wanted and deserved, the work she sought.

The others, I felt, were thriving. True, Izzy had entered my life like a bomb—a bomb I loved from the first—and needed grounding and calming, basic obedience commands. He needed them so badly that I couldn't fail to provide them if we were going to coexist. So I did. He was also keen to work with sheep, I soon learned, and he was shockingly good at it.

Rose remained the lead farm dog, an indispensable part of life in Bedlam. She was living the life she was meant for, doing the jobs this storied breed needed and loved to do.

Pearl was a house dog. Her bad legs made too much time outside difficult, even dangerous. So she was delighted merely to go for a few walks, accompany me on my farm rounds, hang around Paula and me, go to readings and therapy appointments (mine and her own), and doze by the window or on the front porch the rest of the time.

But what about Clementine? She was a sunshiney dog, always apparently happy and waggling; you could hardly look at her and not brighten. Still, I began noticing how often she wanted to come along but couldn't, how often I saw her sweet face peering through a gate or window, heard her whining softly because we were off for an errand that didn't include her.

THE IRONY WAS THAT I'D NEVER WORKED HARDER AT CHOOSING and getting a dog than I had with Clem. I was present right after the litter was born, visited Pam Leslie's kennels twice a week for the first two months, consulted with behaviorists about the puppies' emerging characteristics and personality.

I worked hard to pick the right one for me, and I succeeded. Clem was not the kind of dog who challenged humans in the way Orson, Izzy, or even Rose did. I'd sometimes been drawn to troubled dogs that needed help, but Clem (apart from her predictable Lab proclivity for rolling in mud and eating gross things) caused little or no trouble.

She was cheerful, loved to chase a ball a few times a day, rode happily along in the truck, visited the garden center and hardware stores, sat quietly at parades, even at fireworks displays.

I've written before of the drama of the Good Dog. Trainers know to pay special attention to good dogs, because they're the ones their owners pay less attention to, mostly because they don't demand much. The more dogs there are—especially the more troubled ones—the more the good dogs can fade into the background.

Clem had become my canine sweetheart, the only dog who slept in my bed, who shared my couch, often with her head in my lap. I loved her dearly.

She was definitely not a dog—as border collies tend to be— that forms powerful attachments to only one human and shuts out the rest of the world. The Whore of Bedlam was close to many people, particularly anyone holding a biscuit. Her universal lovingness and acceptance were perhaps the things I most cherished about her.

But it also led me to start thinking not only about whether she deserved more, but whether she could adapt fairly easily to some other arrangement.

I KNOW SOME OF MY DOG-RELATED PHILOSOPHIES ARE INCOMPREHENSIBLE, even anathema, to many other dog owners and lovers.

I can't, for example, subscribe to the notion that the acquisition of every dog represents a lifetime commitment, a bond that must never be altered or broken. Adaptability is one of dogs' greatest traits. Yet the epidemic personification of dogs— seeing them as children with human-like emotions, and therefore human-like attachment and separation issues—keeps many a dog from a better life.

Mine is hardly an unheard-of analysis. Many breeders and others who work with dogs professionally share it. But it's become almost a cultural taboo to even contemplate giving a dog a better life if that means a life with someone else.

I do contemplate it, especially since I don't believe that dogs possess much self-awareness or consciousness, despite a growing belief to the contrary. They're probably more intelligent than cows, and far more attached to people than sheep, but, like the other animals on the farm, they live in the moment, largely by instinct. They won't spend much time feeling miserable if a new owner provides affection, recreation, health care—and dinner.

I don't believe it admirable or even ethical to keep violent dogs especially near human beings. I don't believe in taking extraordinary measures to keep dogs alive beyond their natural spans, not in a world where few humans have basic health care.

I do believe that it's not only appropriate but our solemn obligation to give our dogs the best possible lives, even if it means finding another place for them to live.

So here I was, on the horns of yet another dog dilemma. I had already given one dog away. I'd put down Orson, my beloved soulmate, and two ailing Labs. And now I was considering a different arrangement for Clementine, not because I didn't love her, but because I loved her so much.

"People will not forgive you," a friend in New York City warned. "They'll think it callous. They'll wonder if you see dogs as disposable."

That's not my concern. I have to do what benefits the dog. Loving a dog doesn't just mean clinging to it, regardless of circumstances. It sometimes means stepping back to be certain you've done well by these wondrous creatures, done the best you can.

I was feeling overwhelmed. My back problems had limited what I could do in a day. My writing career was growing increasingly demanding. I traveled more, spoke more, wrote more. The farm had expanded, and its population grown.

Great dogs deserve great lives, but I feared Clem wasn't having one.

Still, giving her away didn't feel like an option. I'd worked too hard to choose and train her. She was Paula's favorite dog. I loved her too much.

ALI WAS A PHYSICAL THERAPIST AT THE CENTER WHERE I WAS BEING treated. Though I usually brought Pearl to my sessions, now and then I brought Clem instead, to make her feel less left out.

Ali and I started talking dogs, and we kept on talking dogs. Ali wanted one badly and was scouring shelters, reading books, talking to clients. She asked me about breeds and trainers. I warned about how important I thought it was for people to imagine the dog they want, research carefully, and choose dogs they're likely to love that also mesh with their lives. I told her people got dogs in such a hit-or-miss way that many ended up ignored, abandoned, dead, or in shelters.

Ali was a prime candidate for dog ownership. In her thirties, deeply committed to her work, she made her own hours, scheduling as many patients as she wanted to see, in a place we already knew a well-behaved dog might be welcome. Outside work, she was athletic, a hiker and runner, soccer and lacrosse player. She lived alone, in a house close to ponds, mountain trails, deep woods.

Her dog could be with her day and night, at work, at games, jogging along with her for short distances, swimming with her.

She wanted a dog that loved people, that was reliable with kids, that was happy to be active but could also settle down. A yellow Lab, she told me, like a healthier Pearl, or like Clem. That's when the idea first hit me: Perhaps there was a way we could all get what we wanted. I could have less chaos; Ali could have a wonderful dog; Clem could have a great life.

I mulled the prospect over for a couple of months, during which I checked Ali out, watched her at the therapy center, took Clem more often so they could get to know each other. Then I proposed that Clem and Ali spend a weekend or two together. I described this as a way Ali could experience life-with-dog before making a commitment, but I think we both knew that I was suggesting something potentially more serious than an occasional visit.

Even this first overture was difficult; I felt sorrow and loss as I contemplated it. I worried that Clem would be anxious and

confused, that I would deeply regret not having her sweet, enthusiastic presence every day. My heart sank simply at the
growing complexity of my life, at my rebellious spine, at my inability to just let things be and look the other way. Clem was
not, in any sense of the term, suffering. Still, I couldn't shake the
uneasy sense that it was a travesty to squeeze a dog like this in
among other dogs, growing commitments, new limitations. It
wasn't a loving way to treat a dog but a selfish one.

That first weekend, I drove Clem to the therapy center and
dropped her off with a bag of rawhide chews, dog food, toys,
and treats. I gave Ali a long list of careful instructions.

I called half a dozen times to see how they were doing together. I'd warned Ali that Clem might be anxious or restless,
might even run off looking for me or the other dogs or the
farm.

It was a few hours before Ali called back. "What a great
dog," she bubbled. "She's so sweet and well trained, and so
much fun. We are worn out. We just got back from the pond;
she chased her water ball for half an hour. Then we hiked
through the woods for a couple of miles. We went to my soccer game, and people took turns sitting with her, holding her
leash. She made a million friends."

A line had formed, Ali reported—players and spectators,
kids and adults and passersby, all waiting to pat Clem, hold her
leash, walk her, toss a ball. "She didn't want to leave."

Oh. I'd been prepared to offer advice on how to calm troubled dogs.

"I cooked a little hamburger and mixed it with her food,
like you recommended. She ate it all, did her business," Ali went
on. "I'm just crazy about her. I want her with me every minute
that's possible, and that you're comfortable with. This is the dog
I've been dreaming of, but I don't want to take away your dog.
I want you to be okay about her visiting with me."

To say the least, I had mixed feelings. I was frankly a bit surprised that Clem hadn't undergone a few hours of anxiety at this transition—the way I had. Yet Clem was clearly doing well and getting plenty of the stuff she loved: one-on-one attention, varied physical activity, healthy doses of everything from an adoring public to swimming. Much more than I could provide on a daily basis.

Maybe this didn't have to be so stark a choice, so painful a drama. I could do something that would spread much joy—and offer Ali joint custody. Clem could divide her time between Ali's house and my farm, only a forty-minute ride away.

I didn't have to give her away and not see her anymore. I could set up an arrangement that would bring happiness to a worthy and loving human, provide an active and delightful life for a great dog, and still give me and Paula and my dogs the gift of time with Clem for substantial periods.

So we did it. Ali and I have joint custody, and Clementine has two devoted and loving caretakers. We discuss her health care; agree on food, diet, and exercise; trade Clem stories. Both of us—all of us—shower this dog with love, attention, fine treats, and exercise.

A week after Clem first went to stay with Ali, I had my usual physical therapy appointment. Ali offered to bring Clem to the center, as she would from time to time, if I wanted to see her.

Of course, I said. I was concerned that Clem have enough time to bond with Ali before she saw me again, but from what I was hearing, that had already happened. I brought Pearl along, and Paula, who was eager to check on her favorite dog.

Clem was thrilled to see all of us. She chewed on Pearl, jumped up and licked me, and tore madly around the room for five or six minutes.

Even though she would be back with us in just a week or

so, while Ali took a long-planned vacation, the encounter felt a little strange. Clem seemed very attached to Ali, following her when she walked behind the desk or over to a table, but then confused, running over to me, then back to Ali again. She was all over Pearl, too, licking and sniffing her.

She seemed excited and nervous, a perfectly natural behavior given the circumstances, but it was also a bit uncomfortable to see. Had I upset her stable existence, threatened her equilibrium?

She and Ali were clearly very attached to each other, but she was still also attached to me and to Pearl and, I'm sure, the other dogs. She greeted Paula just as enthusiastically, wriggling and licking.

Still, it had only been a week. Paula and I both felt a stab when we left—without Clem—but I was pretty convinced the new configuration might serve everyone.

Later, when I checked in with Ali, she told me that Clem had taken a nap just after we left. Then they'd gone out to chase some balls and had a swim.

"She's had a fabulous day," Ali said. "She's asleep on my lap right now."

A few weeks later, Clem seemed delighted with the arrangement. She was happy to come here for a few days, excited to see me and my dogs, and just as excited to see Ali when she came to pick her up again.

Ali and Clem never had a moment's discomfort, not in the first hour, the first night, or the first week. Before very long, Clem seemed to grasp this was her human, in the same way I knew Izzy was my dog.

Some of the matchmaking had been obvious. Ali was available, loving, and patient, with an easy, calm demeanor. She knew how to make her wishes clear in a consistent yet affectionate way.

Clem was a dog that needed to be physically close to people. Ali made a spot on the sofa for her, and invited her into bed at night.

Clem liked to go places, and Ali could bring her nearly everywhere—to work, to games, to visits with her family and friends.

Clem loved bounding through the woods and swimming, and there were woods and ponds and streams all around Ali's house.

Clem craved the focused, one-on-one attention of a human, and Ali, living alone, wanted a companion to share her life and love of the outdoors. Both were athletes. Both were loving, outgoing, enthusiastic, and remarkably good-natured.

I do think that over the next few years, Clem's time with me will diminish as I grow older, my work and the farm make their demands, and other animals, perhaps even other dogs, come and go. Ali will be with Clem day and night, all week long. We'll have our visits—when Ali travels, Clem will always come to the farm, for instance—but I know Clementine. She'll make many friends in her new world and grow to love them. They'll want to spend time with her, and they will be a closer, more regular part of her life than I.

Meanwhile, Izzy and I were bonding more by the day. Rose could not be busier, more competent or appreciated. Pearl was a nuclear love reactor who spent much of her day on laps or on her back, getting her belly scratched. I yelled less, and training grew easier, calmer, more productive. It was simpler to manage two busy border collies when the only other dog was Perfect Pearl.

Clem could not stay happily suspended between these two worlds for long, I understood. She would attach more to one person than the other, and I knew which one it would be. This was a loss of my own making. That it seemed justified, the right choice, didn't mean that it felt easy or pain-free.

In fact, when I looked ahead, I felt extraordinarily sad, and my heart sank almost into my belly. Little Clem, who crawled onto my shoulder when she was eight weeks old and went to sleep, would one day be someone else's dog.

But that, to me, was the wonder of dogs, that cycle of gain, loss, drama, death, happiness, and love, a song that never stops, that plays over and over. Sometimes the song is joyous, sometimes wrenching, often both.

For now, there was joint custody. Clem was here quite a bit, moving with striking ease between one sphere and the other. She affirmed my deeply held belief about dogs: Their dominant trait, their special genius, is their adaptability.

On a June evening, as the Yankees were getting thumped, Izzy was lying under my feet. Pearl was snoring loudly on her L. L. Bean dog bed. Rose was off in some distant corner of the house, no doubt peering out windows to check on her sheep. And I was alone on the sofa.

My Yankee buddy was gone, sprawled on someone else's couch, licking someone else's face, cadging someone else's snacks, sharing someone else's life. It still felt strange, and it still felt right.

The Quiet Group

FIFTEEN

The Quiet Group

THE LETTER CAME ON A THURSDAY, IN A PLAIN WHITE ENVELOPE sandwiched between circulars full of grocery coupons. I almost threw it away, but the typewritten address caught my eye. I slit the envelope carefully, using a kitchen knife. I couldn't remember the last time I'd received a letter written on a typewriter.

It was composed by someone with excellent grammar, spotless typing, knowledge of the proper format for correspondence as once taught in schools.

Margaret Wheatley said she lived "just a few hills over" from me. She was writing, she said, because she didn't want to bother me with a telephone call or intrude with an unplanned visit.

I hadn't even seen a typewriter for twenty years and could barely remember the last time I used one. (I'd started my first book, a novel, on a typewriter in the late 1980s, then switched midstream to one of the early Apples, and haven't looked back.)

I appreciated Margaret's sensitivity. Privacy and freedom are among the things people most cherish about living in the country, so locals are very careful about intruding. My friends and neighbors never come by without calling first. Disturbingly, however, people from farther away pull into the driveway all the time, along with an occasional tour van, families on outings and reunions, even—in June—an entire wedding party, hoping to pose for a photo session next to the barn.

Margaret's letter:

"I live on Manley Hill, just a few hills over, west of Patterson Hill. In June I will have three visitors, lady friends from 50-plus years ago when we all lived in the Katonah, New York, area."

Most were widowed ("as am I," Margaret wrote), grandmothers and great-grandmothers "still interested in many learning experiences." Also, dog lovers.

She was wondering, Margaret continued, "if we might visit your farm for a short time one day in June. They will be here on the 13th and 14th.

"We have all enjoyed your books. We are a quiet group!

"Thank you for considering my request."

I called Margaret, who was pleased, and surprised, to hear from me. "I didn't think you would call," she said. "I wouldn't if I were you."

Why not? I asked.

"Because you'll get a reputation as a place old ladies will want to visit, and then you'll never have peace or get your books written."

The women had met decades ago, she told me. Margaret,

Karen, Diana, and June. Neighbors and Girl Scout leaders, they'd since scattered around the region, but had stayed friends all these decades and convened annually for trips and treks—hiking and canoeing at first, now less strenuous outings.

Jane, the fifth member of what I'd taken to calling—at least to myself—the Quiet Group, was ill, and it was unclear whether she'd be joining the others.

I was moved by their friendship and faithfulness, the love these women had for one another. I also had a growing sense, though Margaret didn't explicitly say so, that this might be one of their last gatherings.

I also felt a pang for myself and other men. This wasn't something members of my gender were likely to do. My early friends had drifted away, victims of neglect and busyness, or been left behind.

And it was impressive that at an age when some of her peers were fleeing to Florida, Margaret and her friends were out trawling for new experiences. I suppose I identified with that.

The request itself was affecting. I'd never lived in a place people would so want to visit that it qualified as a destination, an adventure. Yet I'd worked hard to make the farm that kind of place, so that people who came here would feel welcome, even uplifted. The dogs and other animals had become veteran ambassadors. I suspected there would come a time—and not far off—when I couldn't be as hospitable, for various reasons, but I didn't relish its coming.

"I would be honored to have you come to the farm," I told her. "What can I prepare for you?"

Nothing, she said, adding, "We don't mean to overstay or be a bother." But as she thought about it, "Perhaps some of us will need some juice, if that wouldn't be a problem."

I imagined she was thinking especially about Jane, if she could be persuaded to come. The group might need refreshment, literally.

I began preparations. Usually, I just walk visitors across the farm, perhaps have Rose push a few sheep around. But the Quiet Group deserved more. I even drew up a rough itinerary, an unprecedented move for someone whose life validated Chaos Theory:

10:30   Arrival. I'd have the group park in the side driveway and enter through the front yard, the only level part of the farm. Introductions of humans and dogs.

Next   Tour of restored Dog Room and living room. I wanted to show off the antique library panels Anthony had hand-hewn, the plaster rosettes he'd laboriously designed and molded, the old wallpaper preserved in some of the panels. I thought the group might appreciate this nod to the past.

Elevenish   Walk out back, meet the donkeys (I'd have them near the barnyard fence, close to the house), distribute carrots and donkey cookies. My guests would likely enjoy the adorable Jesus, who'd grown waist-high but still followed people around like a Lab puppy.

11:15   Come inside the barn to see the restoration, still under way. The work had been painstaking and backbreaking for Anthony and his helper, Ben—days of hammering, sawing, hauling planks and stones around under a broiling sun. The original posts and beams and slate roof remained, but there was new pine siding and windows and a stone foundation.

Anthony, resourceful as always, had located some old windows and built them into the siding, so that the rare interior silo would be visible from the outside. The effect, as with many products of Anthony's burgeoning design instincts, was striking, an old barn with an eclectic touch.

11:30 Meet Elvis and Luna—through the fence. I decided not to bring the Quiet Group into the rear pasture, as Elvis could get overly affectionate in his delight at seeing new people. I wasn't sure the Quiet Group would enjoy being slurped by his enormous tongue, or bumped or jostled.

Next Herding demonstration, starring Rose, with a brief appearance by Izzy.

Finally We'd all sit on the porch, have juice, rest, talk for a while.

I made lunch reservations for the Quiet Group at the funky old German restaurant in nearby Salem called Steininger's, famous for thick croissant sandwiches, fabulous desserts, and homemade chocolates.

Although I was slow to realize it, the pending visit began to take on the cast of a community event. I'd asked Annie to come by in case I needed help with the animals, and she quickly volunteered to bake human cookies to serve with the juice. Meg Southerland at Gardenworks, the stylish local farm and garden center, offered to show the group her vast studio of dried flowers and to make some small arrangements for the ladies if they stopped en route to the restaurant.

Anthony said he'd be by to answer questions about the house or barn restorations. And my friend Maria Heinrich, who painstakingly restores old homesteads with her husband,

Bill, and consequently spends considerable time asking elders for their memories of farms and houses, would also come to meet Margaret and her friends.

Peter Hanks would document the occasion and make copies of photos I could send the visitors as souvenirs.

I was surprised and pleased at how many people wanted to lend a hand. I hadn't had these kinds of friends, this sort of community, before. Over and over, I was learning that dogs and other animals didn't isolate me from people but connected me.

AT PRECISELY 10:30 A.M. ON JUNE 13 A VOLVO STATION WAGON pulled into the driveway and four members of the Quiet Group slowly climbed out.

I spotted Margaret right away—tall, thin, dignified—because she seemed to have stepped right out of her properly composed letter. Two of the women were toting carrots for the donkeys, another biscuits for the dogs.

Though they hardly needed to bring bribes. Rose woofed, but Pearl, Izzy, and Clementine (in residence while Ali was out of town) all came thundering over to the fence, tails wagging, and soon were getting hugs and pats from over the fence.

The visitors seemed an affluent bunch, trim and alert, wearing well-made cotton clothing and cropped hair in various shades of gunmetal and silver. They ranged in age from seventy-four to eighty-six, Margaret had told me, though, oddly, you couldn't really tell who was the senior member and who the young whippersnapper. But their connection to one another, their long shared history of love and unwavering support, was something you could almost see and touch.

We all gathered in the yard to say hello, to establish who was who and who lived where, which was the shy member of the group and which the self-described "talker."

Their early histories were shared: families downstate, Girl Scout troops, camping trips. Then, as their kids grew up and left Girl Scouts behind, "life intervened," as Diana put it. They moved; their families expanded to include in-laws and grand-kids and now great-grandkids (eight among them).

Some of the women had worked outside the home—as an occupational therapist, an office manager, a substitute teacher—and some never had.

Now one lived in Maine, another in New Hampshire, two in Massachusetts, and Margaret a few hills over. But they'd vowed to stay in touch and reassemble at least once a year.

Like long-married couples, they knew the endings to one another's stories, rolled their eyes in advance at the punch lines of often-told jokes. I'd expected to feel sympathy for them, an-ticipating weariness and frailty. Instead, finding them lively, funny, and energetic, I was envious. These were interesting peo-ple, quick and curious. They weren't even all that quiet, I pointed out, causing a whoop of laughter.

"We've been hiking, canoeing, sailing, climbing, all sorts of things in all sorts of places," Margaret summarized airily. There was that time their boat capsized during a thunderstorm and the time a woman in a remote farmhouse threatened to shoot them when they'd wandered off a hiking trail in New Hamp-shire. They'd gotten lost, drenched, nearly frozen.

If the Quiet Group had a leader, Margaret seemed to qual-ify. She spoke softly but was listened to when she did. She had a calm graciousness about her—a grace—that was pro-nounced.

Two or three times, especially a while back, "we let the men come," Margaret added. "They got along quite well, especially on camping trips, when they could have a good time pitching tents and fishing and grilling things."

It was fine, even fun, but it wasn't the same when the men came, June chimed in. So from the 1970s on, they weren't invited. And now, I thought, it really wasn't an option.

"You can't help but be inhibited around men. They just don't talk as openly about things as we do," June explained. "This was *our* time. We needed to be able to confide in each other."

Not once in all those years, Karen added, had the group failed to come to one another's side when there was trouble. And of course there was trouble.

Most of their husbands had died, including Margaret's several years earlier. One was a suicide. There were divorces and losses among the children. They'd cared for their own faltering parents. A house had burned down. There were more prosaic crises and dramas—car accidents, job troubles, financial pressures.

"There was," Margaret said succinctly, "life."

AT FIRST, MY ITINERARY HELD UP.

We began the visit by walking around the house, where the ladies exclaimed happily over my various restoration projects and tactfully refrained from remarking on the preponderance of dog crates and beds and other less gracious elements of decor.

Then we went out to see the animals. Heading toward the barn, I asked June, moving briskly along in her sensible shoes (while I struggled to keep up with my walking stick), how many children she had. She paused and said she had "two living." Her oldest son, she said, had been killed in an avalanche while hiking in Europe.

"They never found his body. He's still up there on the mountain," she said. "My friends have never forgotten him. They're almost the only people who still say his name."

They'd all suffered losses, she added, as if to ward off any sense of self-pity. Diana's boy had left college and simply vanished many years ago. "She's never heard from him, doesn't know if he is dead or alive," June said.

Margaret and her husband, Gilbert, had been an unusual couple, she went on, so loving and happy. "They just enjoyed every moment they spent together," she said.

"Margaret rarely shows it, but she was shattered by Gil's death. Now she seems determined to live in that house forever, even though we all think it's too big."

I remembered Margaret telling me on the phone how much she loved her farmhouse, how she'd shared too brief a time there with a "sweet, wonderful man." Maybe it wasn't too big.

And this year, for the first time any of them could recall, only four women were getting together, not five. "Jane is receiving radiation treatment," said Margaret, who'd drawn alongside us. "We wanted her to come anyway, but she's so tired and she was afraid she'd hold us back. We've always done such active things and we couldn't persuade her that it was all right if she just sat and watched."

The donkeys were pleased to meet the group, and vice versa; the women especially cooed over Jesus.

"You all seem so upbeat," I said, still reeling a bit from hearing the cumulative saga of five decades.

"We are not whiners or complainers," Margaret declared.

"We have all had good and lucky lives—husbands, children, great-grandchildren—and of course we've had each other. We have little to complain about."

She turned to me, gave my shoulder a squeeze. "What a lovely farm. You seem so happy here, and proud. You are wonderful to invite all these old ladies here."

No, I thought, they were wonderful. I was merely lucky to be their host.

THE TOUR CONTINUED INTO THE BARN, WHERE KAREN CONFIDED that she sensed "negative energy," a remark that triggered eye-rolling from Diana, "the practical one."

"I don't have much truck with spirits," Diana announced. "I believe what I can see."

Karen snorted. "That's why we don't include her in our spiritual discussions," she said. "She's much too hardheaded.

"Never mind her," Karen insisted. "Something bad happened in that barn. Perhaps somebody died there. You need to take care of it." When I told her I was fantasizing about moving my office into the hayloft one day, she was even more insistent that I rid the place of whatever unpleasant reverberations she was picking up. She was pleased to hear that I had a consulting shaman who could probably assist.

We filed back outside. Elvis, beginning to connect the idea of people and goodies, came over to the back gate and allowed everyone to scratch his enormous nose as he inhaled apples.

Then Rose did her work and zipped up the hill, pushing the sheep ahead of her into the training pen, to a round of admiring applause. She was uncharacteristically friendly afterward, joining us on the porch and giving each of the women a quick lick before darting off to observe from her favorite spot deep in the garden.

Izzy, too, had shown off his still-rudimentary herding skills, circling the sheep in their pen. He was evolving into a lovebug, sticking his nose into everybody's hand for scratching, staring into people's eyes.

But no animal can really outshine Pearl when it comes to working a crowd, one by one. Leaning into the women, she swooned over onto her back for scratching and hugging. Those eyes can penetrate almost any heart.

A LITTLE LATER, SITTING ON THE PORCH, I WONDERED WHERE ANthony had gotten to. Annie and Maria were passing juice and cookies, and the Quiet Group were all sitting in Adirondack chairs and rockers, patting Pearl's head and scratching her belly. But Anthony was MIA.

So when my phone rang and I saw his cell number pop up on the caller ID, I knew something was wrong. "What's up?" I asked.

"It's Mo," he said, sounding agitated. "We're up at my house"—meaning the one he was building a half mile up the road—"and he's disappeared. I've been looking and calling and I can't find him."

Mo, Anthony's black Lab, spent many of his days on my farm, hanging around with my dogs while Anthony was working, staying with me when he and Holly went away. Mo was easy to have around, obedient and friendly, able to slip happily into farm life.

And he never ran off. Mo was a "ride-along" dog who accompanied Anthony on his travels. Like his buddy Clementine,

Mo might veer off to roll in deer scat or devour a carcass, but he never disappeared or refused to respond to calls.

"I'm on my way," I said. So much for my itinerary.

I explained the crisis to the Quiet Group, excused myself, and yelled for Rose, who jumped into the car. She knew when it was time to work.

Country dogs like Mo, however mellow, did face certain perils. They might encounter old fences—tangles of rusting barbwire—or plunge into ravines. Sometimes their collars snagged on tree limbs and they couldn't wriggle free.

Anthony had been running around in the heat for nearly an hour; he knew better than I that Mo would normally have responded if he could.

We pulled up behind the house, still largely a construction site. Anthony was somewhere out in the brush, yelling for his dog.

"Rose," I said in the voice I used when we were herding, "get Mo! Find Mo!" I have a nearly unshakable faith that Rose grasps the idea behind odd commands, even if she doesn't precisely understand what I'm saying.

"C'mon, Rosie, find Mo," I said, and I watched as this skinny, thirty-six-pound sprite, all energy and instinct, began circling Anthony's truck, parked by the house.

She picked up a scent, ran down the hill and back, then, pausing and raising her ears, charged up behind the house. She knew Mo's name, but even if she couldn't precisely understand my language, it was in her nature to track creatures in motion. That was how she kept track of sheep. If Mo was running around out there, Rosie, with her acute hearing and sense of smell, might pick up on it.

She certainly seemed to be after something. I clambered laboriously, painfully, up the steep incline behind her.

She was well ahead of me, barely visible through the scrub, looking down into a shallow gully, where I saw her biting and pulling at something. Suddenly, amid the sound of crackling branches and ripping vines, up popped Mo, shaking himself free of the thick undergrowth. He came bounding toward me, panting heavily. I had no doubt that he'd gotten stuck.

I called Anthony on his cell and told him Rose had found Mo and that we'd leave him in his truck. I could hear relief and exhaustion in Anthony's voice. Then we zipped back down the hill and I flashed the V-for-victory sign to my visitors on the porch, to cheers and applause.

"You are my hero," I told Rose for the umpteenth time, kissing her nose.

We had apparently not been missed much. My friends had simply taken over the hosting duties, a smooth transition. Maria and Annie were yakking with Margaret, Karen, June, and Diana as if I'd never left, discussing work, men, shamanism, and animals. "We never have trouble finding things to talk about," said Margaret.

It felt nice that this group, friends and newcomers, old and young, could be so at ease with or without me. There was a multigenerational female thing going on, and for a moment I felt in a familiar position, standing outside yet another tent.

In my experience, there's often a sad loneliness about men, a tendency to push critical things—friendship, love, peace of mind—aside.

The Quiet Group knew better, and always had. "Nothing is more important than this," June said softly to me, as the others were arguing about the spirits in the barn. "It isn't that we love each other more than our families, not at all. But we all understood, from the beginning, how sustaining friendship can be."

It had taken me much longer to learn that lesson. I felt

lucky to have finally gotten it at all. Annie and Maria were decades younger, but I sensed great respect between these generations. The dogs served dutifully as ambassadors, shuttling back and forth, reveling in the attention, the hugs, the occasional cookie crumb that dropped to the floor.

I thought I could actually feel the energy these women were talking about. As the conversation shifted easily—how much June loved seeing Elvis the steer, how impressed Diana was with the remarkable Rose, how Karen was picking up odd vibes—Margaret was beaming at the way this long-treasured tradition was unfolding once more. I could see, too, the pleasure Annie and Maria took in meeting these elders, perhaps envisioning their own futures, the connections they'd forged themselves and those that might lie ahead.

A half hour later, as if through some invisible signal, the ladies moved to leave. They had other stops to make.

As they walked down the porch steps, across the lawn toward the car, Karen turned to me.

"Thank you for this," she said quietly. "This is such a gift. You and your farm have brought us joy, more than perhaps you know." I offered my hand, but she gave me a gentle hug. I didn't know precisely what she meant.

I drove ahead, leading the way to Gardenworks, where the ever-gracious Meg and her workers were waiting to greet the Quiet Group with more refreshments, a look at Meg's gardens and flower-arranging facilities. Meg had assembled four baskets of dried flowers, and a fifth to be taken back to Jane. I'd offered to pay for these gifts, but of course Meg had refused to take any money.

Afterward, following another round of hugs and kisses and good-byes, I was sorry to see them drive off into town for lunch. I could likely see Margaret again, since she lived nearby, but I doubted I'd see the others. I wasn't even certain they'd see each other. By now, you couldn't help noticing the limps, the fatigue, the slowing pace.

Life imposed its own limits, even on women of such energy and grace. I hoped I could age so well.

BACK AT THE FARM, I GATHERED THE DOGS AND CALLED THEM ALL into the pasture, where the donkeys came sidling up, and Mother paused in her savage patrols to stick her head out the barn door. Elvis and Luna watched from the other side of the fence.

I wanted my peeps around me, a comforting collective presence as I distributed pats and ear scratches, apples and carrots. I was glad for their company, grateful for their good natures. I collected a fresh egg from the hens' nesting box.

Then I called the dogs and we went into the house.

Rose

SIXTEEN

Lifetime Dogs

FOR HIS FIRST THREE YEARS, IZZY HAD LIVED WITH ANOTHER BOR-
der collie in a small, specially built doghouse encircled by a sizable fence. All day long, he ran along its perimeter, the
caretaker's own border collie running with him on the outside.

Aside from that routine, or compulsion, Izzy did no work,
took no walks, had no training, saw very few people, not even
a vet. He'd never ridden in a car. He was by no means abused,
in the classic sense: He had shelter and food and when the
weather was brutally cold, the caretaker allowed him a few
nights in his house, since the doghouse was unheated.

But his only real human connection was with Flo, the animal lover who visited regularly and worried about him. (She
was blond-haired, and he still exults whenever he meets a
blonde.)

When I brought him home, Izzy was truly frantic, excited and aroused, with no outlet for all that energy and drive. A border collie without work is a confused and disoriented creature. He didn't know any commands. He didn't even know his name.

Two months later, I pulled into a PetSmart in Saratoga Springs to pick up some dog food. For the first dozen or so times Izzy rode in my car, he threw up. Now, like most border collies, he loved to ride shotgun and hopped into the car even when he wasn't invited.

We got out, crossed the crowded parking lot, walked into the store. Izzy had rarely been indoors before he came to me, let alone in a mall superstore. This one was full of carts, an ASPCA animal adoption fair, birds and reptiles, and throngs of shoppers.

I was on a book deadline, lost in thought about a section I was wrestling with, and I'm embarrassed to admit that I didn't realize until we both were inside that I hadn't put Izzy on a leash.

This was both careless and irresponsible—he could have run off, panicked, tangled with another shopper's dog, gotten hit by a car in the lot—yet completely unintentional. Izzy was so automatically by my side at the farm, in or out of the house, that I almost never used a leash.

Although he was responding amazingly well to training, I hadn't in any way prepared him for this stimulating new environment with its numerous canine distractions—bins of pigs' ears and biscuits and toys and balls, other animals, strange people.

The odd thing was, the reason I didn't think about a leash was that Izzy was walking right alongside me as usual, behind the cart I was pushing. He barely looked at other dogs, didn't sniff any of the goodies. A number of salespeople and customers stopped to admire and pet him, and he accepted their compliments calmly. Eventually, somebody said, "My goodness, he isn't even on a leash! What a good boy!" Yikes, I thought, what a dumb human.

There were, of course, plenty of leashes at PetSmart, so I grabbed one and put it in my cart. But I didn't slip it onto his collar right away; intrigued, I decided to give him a chance to simply stay by my side. We passed three poodles and a rottweiler and Izzy sniffed one and ignored the others.

More people stopped to hug and pet him. He loved the attention. Izzy was curious with people, appreciative but not demonstrative. He never licked me; he simply closed his eyes and waited to be touched.

He was a loving, even sensual creature, but only indirectly. He was what some behaviorists call a "propinquity dog": he was always by my side. I patted him and scratched him behind the ears, but our closeness—growing hourly—mostly involved just being with each other.

I loaded the cart with big bags of food and headed for the cashier. Izzy walked alongside, took a biscuit from the cashier, then followed me and the cart outside. I did put the leash on in the parking lot, but despite all the vehicles, kids, and dogs, he never so much as stepped away. He merely hopped into the car and sat on the passenger side, as if he'd been riding along for a hundred years.

I had a sudden flashback to the day he'd seen the donkeys and fled all the way to Cossayuna. For days thereafter, he looked at me as if I were a strange creature dropped from the sky. Now he stayed glued to my leg, as comfortable in a mall as in our living room.

After a few more weeks, I got the strange feeling that Izzy

had been waiting for me those years he was alone, running around in circles; that he'd been expecting me. And that when he met me, saw where and how I lived, it was almost as if he'd already envisioned it and could slip seamlessly into the picture.

I knew that none of this reverie could possibly be so. Yet it seemed true, especially when he looked at me and cocked his head, studying me like a canine archaeologist who'd happened upon an odd artifact.

Ever since I began writing about dogs, I've asked people whether they had a "lifetime dog." It's surprising how many people know what I mean without any explanation. Breeders, trainers, behaviorists, rescuers, ordinary dog lovers—almost everyone could readily name such a dog (or cat or horse).

To me, a lifetime dog is the one that enters your life at a particular, critical point and changes or affects you in ways no other animal can or will.

For me, this dog was Orson. No other animal ever had—or, to my mind, ever could have—such extraordinary impact.

But I was beginning to wonder: Could you have more than one lifetime dog?

Izzy turned out to be a very different dog from the one I'd first seen tearing around his odd little compound.

By turns frightened, confused, and frantic for his first few weeks, he initially did an enormous amount of damage in the house. Had I not been through this before, not lived with border collies for years, not experienced similar dramas with Orson, I would surely have found another home for him, pronto.

But because of Orson, I knew Izzy would come through this period, and I believed I'd learned enough to help him.

Most of the time, I managed to stay calm, patient, affectionate, and clear. It was probably the first time I'd responded so evenly to so challenging a creature. There is, I thought, some benefit to growing older.

I was right: Once Izzy experienced something for a few days—mangleproof crates, new commands, a tribe of donkeys, life in a house, eliminating outside that house—he was not troubled by it again. He paid close attention to me and my routines, and he learned quickly. Day by day, he grew calmer, easier, more responsive.

One odd thing: He might press his nose into my hand or sit with me for a while on the sofa; and once he could spend the night uncrated, he took up position at the foot of the bed. But he still never licked me.

And so what? Izzy had undergone a dizzying transformation, from a dog with little experience with humans to a dog that acted as if he'd been with me his whole life.

When I rode the ATV, he ran alongside. When I visited the cows, he lay down next to me. When I brushed the once-fearsome donkeys, he was soon stretched out on the grass nearby.

If I went outside to talk to Anthony or Annie, he slipped out the door before it could close and shadowed me, lying down a few inches away as I talked. Whenever I turned around in alarm—a legacy of the years with Orson—and yelled, "Izzy! Where are you?" Anthony or someone else would invariably point to my ankle and say: He's right there next to you.

He herded sheep with me, he lay at my feet when I wrote and under the footstool when I watched TV. He was suddenly my companion through life. It seemed so utterly natural that it was almost bewildering.

I was particularly amazed by the ease and calm with which

he approached the sheep. He moved slowly, nearly tiptoeing in a gorgeous, trial-quality outrun. Sometimes he walked calmly up to the herd and simply lay down, giving the border collie eye. He might lie there fifteen minutes, nearly motionless, until the sheep clustered together and, unnerved, started to move. Then he would nudge the flock along, creeping up slowly behind. Seeing these instincts arise, I'd been working with him each day at the training pen.

Izzy didn't have Rose's focused energy or seasoned farm-dog skills. He wouldn't take on donkeys or cows, which was probably fortunate. But after a few weeks, he'd learned to shift directions when he heard "come bye" and "away to me," and he lay down almost instantly on command.

Elsewhere—in homes, stores, or vets' offices—he simply stayed with me, paying little or no attention to other dogs, unperturbed by dirt bikes, trucks, or school buses.

This dog—a companionable working dog—was obviously already there; it was part of Izzy's makeup. I wasn't skilled enough, I hadn't had him long enough, to have trained him so well. I'd simply provided the right environment, and he had come home.

The other dogs had accepted Izzy with equanimity. His arrival didn't change Rose's life much at all; she got her normal doses of herding and farmwork. Pearl loved Izzy as she loved all living things.

Clem was the one most likely to feel displaced by his suddenly central role in my life, but she licked him and dozed next to him, and he was tolerant of her comings and goings. Curiously, for a strong-willed male (intact when I got him), Izzy never challenged any of the others. He seemed pleased just to join the pack.

. . .

As summer advanced, I began bringing Rose and Izzy out to the sheep together, a supposedly difficult maneuver. Although he was a large and dominant dog, Izzy deferred to Rose in the pasture. When I told her to bring the sheep, he would stay out of her way, lying down while she worked. When she and the herd came toward me, Izzy instinctively got up and "squared off"—moved to the opposite side from her.

It was startling, and exciting, to see the pair of them working with and responding to each other. With Rose on one side and Izzy on the other, the sheep had no choice but to move slowly between them, so that the two dogs could march the sheep along in sync, at my command.

I was delighted to see them doing this ancient work together, and it was a continuing revelation that such skills surfaced in Izzy so quickly. Rose and I had been working together almost daily for three years. I would have expected a dog living alone behind a fence with no training to remain confused and unreliable around sheep for some time, perhaps permanently. Instead, after a few months, he seemed to have grown up here.

I began to wonder whether I could march the flock out of the pasture and across the road using both Rose and Izzy, a herding strategy with the potential to prove either dazzling or disastrous.

One sticky morning, fingers crossed, I tried it. The sheep were at the top of the pasture when I opened the gate and sent Izzy up the hill. They bunched together at his approach (a good sign; they used to run from him). He went into the border collie crouch and crept up the hill next to them, dropped down, lay still. I opened the gate again to let Rose in. As she tore up-hill with lightning speed, Izzy remained motionless.

The sheep had backed into a corner of the pasture fence—a tough position for a dog to dig them out of. But Rose and I had been practicing this procedure for a couple of years. She moved to the left, crawled around behind the flock, glared and nipped at one of the ewes until she moved away from the fence, and then the whole herd followed, trotting down the hill, Rose close behind, Izzy waiting in place.

Once the sheep were well down the hill, I gave him the command to move—"Go, Izzy, get the sheep!" and swung open the main pasture gate.

Rose drove the sheep through it, with Izzy close behind, and flock and dogs went sailing down the driveway, across the road, and into the meadow. Once they were happily grazing, Izzy lay down next to me. I called Rose, and she lay down as well.

We sat and watched for a half hour as the flock tanked up. Then I told Rose and Izzy to bring me the sheep, and we reversed the trek, back across the road, toward the gate. Izzy moved calmly and at some distance, but he was definitely pressuring the sheep to move along as Rose circled around, keeping the flock together.

Once the sheep were safely back in the pasture, I yelled, "That'll do!" and both dogs spun around and came to me, mission accomplished.

I whooped and yelled; a private celebration. There were no judges or ribbons within a hundred miles, but I felt I was finally beginning to learn something about working with dogs. Rose, as always, was mistress of the universe, but Izzy was now a colleague, a fellow herder. He might never be as focused or versatile (then again, he might), but he would certainly be able to herd sheep, no small thing for a border collie. After long years in isolation, this dog was moving into the life he deserved, the work he was bred for, the attention and activity he craved.

So, in a way, was I. If your life changes, can't another lifetime dog appear? I wasn't the same person who'd encountered Orson five years earlier. I'd been through a lot, seen and experienced a lot, assembled this new life. If Orson accompanied me through one passage in my lifetime, perhaps Izzy was going to mark this one.

For me, the jury was still out on the question of whether we can have more than one lifetime dog. It hadn't been long enough. I wasn't sure. There seemed something opportunistic about the designation, as if Orson hadn't really counted and he could be replaced by the next beautiful, troubled border collie that showed up. But some new ideas were percolating in my mind as the dogs and I entered the house.

A few weeks before I'd been arguing with Anthony, insisting that, obviously, you could have a lifetime dog only once in a lifetime. What else did the term mean? He had just as heatedly disagreed. "You can't know that until your life is over."

Back indoors as the sun climbed, Rose went off to keep tabs, out the living room window, on her sheep. Pearl came in from the front yard and was soon snoring contentedly. Izzy darted into the well of the desk, his nose resting against my leg. He drifted off and I went to work.

A few days later I was asleep in bed, with Izzy, as usual, curled at my feet. Sometime before dawn a rainstorm rattling against the old slate roof made me stir. As I opened my eyes, I was surprised to see Izzy, wide awake, lying on the adjacent pillow and staring into my face. He leaned over and licked me gently, once, on my right cheek. I slid my arm across his shoulder and we both went back to sleep.

Dairy barn restoration

SEVENTEEN

Perfect Lives

THE KEY TO SPENDING TIME OUTDOORS, AS JUNE WINDS DOWN AND the true summer heat begins to build, is to be up and out early in the day. You can't outfox the flies and mosquitoes, lying in wait, but you can do the chores, herd the sheep, and squeeze in an ATV ride before you, the dogs, or the flock collapse from heatstroke. So it was just a little past dawn when I peeled the cover off the ATV, pulled out the choke, warmed the engine.

I piloted the machine across the road and along a mile-long path into the woods. We had brush-hogged, mowed, and worn this trail to nowhere in particular. Sometimes we veered off to cut a new one through woods and clearings, up hillsides.

I brought a bowl and a jug of water for the dogs and usually paused two or three times to let them rest and to take in the eerie quiet. I often had the feeling something was watching our little parade; deer and coyotes had left evidence of their presence in the forest.

Rose always took point, running ahead about twenty feet, zipping back and forth, keeping an eye on the ATV and on Izzy and me. Izzy ran alongside, a few feet to the left. I'd never been able to outrun him, nor to tire him out. Pearl's legs couldn't handle this pounding; she stayed behind in the shady yard.

The sun was streaming through the trees and the wisps of early-morning mist as we cut a new path up a steep hill.

It was a sharp slope. The dogs struggled through the underbrush as the hardy machine skittered up to the crest; I wore a helmet and gloves to protect against falls and brambles. When we broke out into a clearing, I was surprised to see that we were now peering down on Bedlam Farm from about two miles away. The farm was looking spiffier these days, thanks to Anthony's handiwork—fresh paint, new stone wall, half of a rebuilt barn.

Both dogs lay down next to me and drank eagerly when I filled their water bowl; I tossed them a couple of strips of beef jerky. The scene brightened my spirits: the woods, the hills, the beams of light streaking through the clouds, my lovely farm nestled below. I could glimpse the sheep and donkeys grazing in the pasture. The quiet—a blend of rustling leaves and birdsong—was one of the most beautiful sounds I've ever heard.

Each dog came up to me to offer licks and get a pat. Border collies to the core, they were also suggesting that rest period was over: time to get back to work. Pearl and Clem would have known how to savor such a moment; they were experts at resting. But not Rose or Izzy.

I called Paula on the cell I'd carried along to wish her good morning; she was back in New Jersey but liked to keep track of me. She could easily imagine me lying semiconscious in the woods somewhere, having turned the ATV over or smacked into a tree. "Be careful going back," she said. "Nobody would find you. Are you wearing your helmet?"

Such a mishap was more likely than she knew; I'd already had a couple of spills.

"I got an e-mail from a woman in Boston this morning," I reported. "She said she'd always wanted to have a farm and live there with her dogs and some animals. She said she envied me, because I had a perfect life."

A WEEK EARLIER, PAULA AND I WERE ABOUT TO CLIMB INTO THE CAR, headed for Saratoga and a rare movie. She hadn't been up for a couple of weeks, and a lot of things were going on that we were eager to talk about on the drive. But as we walked out the back door, I glanced up and saw three donkeys grazing. It set off a minor alarm.

The four donkeys always—always—eat, sleep, play, and graze within a dozen feet of one another. It's a trait they share with sheep—if you see one alone, something is wrong.

I walked up to the pasture to investigate, then came back and told Paula we weren't going anywhere. Jeannette, the oldest donkey, was hobbling, her right leg dangling, evidently so painful she couldn't place it on the ground. I knelt next to her—to my surprise she let me, helped by a couple of cookies that kept her occupied—and took out a hoofpick. I probed to see if a stone or some other object had lodged in her hoof, but I didn't find anything. Her sensitivity was so acute that I suspected an abscess.

I called the large-animal vets and also Ken Norman, the farrier. The vets were out on emergency calls; it might be twenty-four hours before they could come. Ken was thinking abscess as well, but he couldn't get to me until the next day either.

Meanwhile, Jeannette could barely stand. I found the salts the vets had left for me after a previous round, mixed them into a bucket of warm water, and soaked her hoof. Then I affixed a poultice and offered her some grain laced with painkillers and antibiotics. I brought her a bale of hay so she wouldn't have to wander for food.

Then it began to rain, and it took me half an hour to lead poor crippled Jeannette into the shelter of the pole barn. I brought more buckets of salts; I changed her poultice. I still couldn't see the abscess.

In a few hours, I was soaked and muddy and my back was killing me. Worse, Jeannette seemed in even greater pain.

So we didn't see a movie that night, nor did I get much sleep. Nights like that happen at least twenty times a year on the farm, and the pace picks up during lambing season. Donkeys, sheep, cows, and, especially, dogs don't lead static lives. They're forever cutting themselves, eating the wrong thing, developing parasites. One dog or another is always barfing, limping, or bleeding. Elvis has already gotten himself stuck in fences and tangled in buried wires.

When the large-animal vet comes, life becomes even more complex. Donkeys understand what vets are up to and flee, and there's no simple way to make an eighteen-hundred-pound steer stand still for his rabies shot.

So there was nothing unusual or especially dramatic about my night with Jeannette. It happens: Donkeys go lame; cows break through fences. Moreover, these things never seem to happen in pleasant weather.

THE PERFECT LIFE IS LIKE THE PERFECT DOG: NEITHER EXISTS, EXCEPT in the fervid imaginations of humans, whose fantasies often drive their expectations beyond reality. You don't need a farm to have a good life, nor does having one give you a perfect one.

It's never easy or simple to tear yourself away from your culture, your natural environment, your family, and your past. You can never completely reinvent yourself.

Nor is every day in Bedlam pure joy. Loving animals is a fraction of the experience of living with them, an experience shaped by food and water, health care and fences, as much as affectionate nuzzles.

And joy is a fraction of the experience of owning a farm. It's much more about shorting wires and crumbling foundations, bees and termites and carpenter ants, rotting windows and leaky roofs and mice-ravaged insulation. I spend many afternoons on the phone, trying to find people to travel long distances to fix things.

And I'm lucky: I can get good help. Anthony can fix almost anything, and Annie can hold a donkey while I dress its wounds. Anthony's wife, Holly, drives me to readings and radio shows. Paula pays the bills, edits my writing, supports every aspect of my life.

Without these people, my supposedly perfect life would collapse like a punctured balloon. Still, there is plenty of responsibility, trouble, and aggravation.

TAKE THAT NEW BARN.

In early spring Anthony had come by to visit and to see how the giant hay barn next to the house was surviving the runoff from heavy rain and melting snow. It was my favorite building, the one I gazed out at every day while I worked. Its century-old boards, which had seen a lot of winters and sheltered hundreds of animals, had faded to shades of silvery-gray beneath weathered red paint.

The barn's first floor had been used for milking; I'd set up lambing pens there and allowed the donkeys and now the cows to come in out of bad weather. I stored grain and medicines there, too. It had an indoor silo, unusual in barns of that period, a graceful curved structure unused for years.

Upstairs, the barn became a cathedral, soaring to the equivalent of a three-story building. Hay was stacked on the second floor, where sun streamed through two old-fashioned windows and through holes in the planks. In summer, barn swallows darted in and out. When the sun lit up the old post-and-beam ceiling, it looked to me like the Sistine Chapel in its weathered glory.

Anthony was less apt to see the poetry therein. "That barn is about to fall over," he announced, leading me to one corner. The barn's foundation, dry-laid stone, had been assembled many generations ago; subsequently, someone had poured a concrete floor atop it. Water, time, and the heaving caused by heat and cold had cracked the concrete, which was crumbling.

Now the corner of the barn was sagging, the whole building tilting forward. Locals had assured me that it was askew for long years before I arrived and would stand for years to come. Anthony didn't think so.

"We have to fix it up or knock it down," he said. "Otherwise, it will just collapse."

Few barns upstate get restored. It's an expensive proposition, and aluminum sheds are cheaper to buy and easier to maintain.

If my barn was to survive, Anthony explained, it would have to be dismantled and the supports jacked up until the structure was level. Sills had to be rebuilt, new foundations laid, stone walls painstakingly reconstructed, windows replaced. We could probably save and repair its slate roof, but the weathered siding I loved had to come down, to be replaced with new wood.

Doing all this would be another vast, expensive disruption. Anthony and I looked at each other. I couldn't let that venerable barn topple, not if I could preserve it. But I really couldn't afford another pricey undertaking so soon.

I applied for a loan.

Fixing up the old barn would be both a glorious opportunity and a miserable chore, another reminder that the perfect life didn't come easily, cheaply, or without risk.

THERE ARE DAYS WHEN I GET A GLIMPSE OF WHAT IT MIGHT BE LIKE, though.

Ken Norman has been studying equine hooves for years. A big muscular man in his forties, with curly black hair and an easy, seen-it-all manner, he is always warm, funny, perceptive, and unflappable. He drives a converted fire truck with a big light atop the cab and, usually, two or three dogs inside. If the donkeys glimpse him or his truck, they take off, but I'm always glad to see him.

Hoof-trimming is not particularly unpleasant, usually. I lure the donkeys into the barn with grain, slip halters on, and hold them still as Ken stoops, picks up each leg, trims the hooves, and cleans out the inside with his well-used tools.

But since Anthony had already torn apart the barn, Annie and I had gathered the donkeys within the dog fence behind the house. Working on donkeys is much easier in an enclosed space like a barn, where, because they have nowhere to go, they stand fairly patiently while Ken does his work.

This day, however, was a chase. The donkeys ran in circles or hugged the far corners of the fence while Annie, Ken, and I all gave chase. Jeannette, her abscessed hoof especially tender, bucked and kicked. Ken also wanted to work on the baby, Jesus, who, because it was his first time, struggled frantically.

It was a rough morning. We all got bumped and banged. None of my donkeys has ever kicked me, no matter the circumstances, but though they were smallish Sicilians, they were still powerful and willful.

It took two hours to work on three donkeys and find Jeannette's abscess—actually, she had two—drain the infection, clean the wounds, and apply antibiotics. But she almost immediately felt better, and the donkeys, having dragged us all over the yard, sensed the drama concluding and nuzzled up for cookies, carrots, and scratching. They always seemed to know when it was time to run and when it was time to concede graciously.

Annie, Ken, and I sat down at the backyard picnic table to take a break and catch up on the news in the three months since he'd last come by. He talked about how he'd broken an arm and how it was healing. We traded stories about other donkeys we knew, the large-animal vets and their idiosyncrasies, the mysteries of hooves.

Ken seemed to see all his clients as family, and wanted to know how my dogs were, what was Izzy's story, where was Orson. He cuddled with Pearl. (Everyone cuddles with Pearl.) The donkeys, having just dragged him all over the yard, now clustered around calmly, as if they wanted to hear the gossip, too.

"I love what I do," Ken said. "I only wish I had a stronger back." Didn't we all, I nodded. But his work was grinding, particularly punishing. I only had to wrestle donkeys every few months; Ken struggled with horses and donkeys all day long.

I was always impressed with his knowledge of the animals

he treated. He'd gone to a farrier school in Kentucky, he said. Then he'd worked for fifteen years, honing his skills and barn-side manner. Annie peppered him with questions about proper donkey care.

It was a sunny afternoon, but a breeze kept the bugs at bay and cooled the place a bit. There was a curious affection and respect around that picnic table. This, oddly, was a tent that I could crawl inside.

"I like the way you care for these girls," Ken said. "I see some bad things as I drive around, so it's always nice to see such happy and healthy animals."

The bond at the table, I realized, was a love for animals, a sense of good fortune that we were all doing what we loved. The backdrop—a few puffy clouds wafting past the rows of corn growing taller in the valley—wasn't bad, either.

Of course, it was also true that the three of us could barely stand, we were so sore and exhausted, and we were covered in mud and hair and donkey droppings. Pain flashed up and down my back. Annie, also drained, said she couldn't wait to get home and go to sleep.

Was this a perfect life?

What made it so appealing was the mix, the sense of crisis and mystery always around the corner, the challenge and responsibility for these affectionate but dependent creatures, the fulfillment of knowing that they were properly cared for, at least for now.

The most perfect thing about my life was that it wasn't. It couldn't ever be, and that was what made the perfect parts perfect.

Ken and I shook hands and agreed that he'd return in a few months. Annie staggered off to her pickup. I hobbled into the house for an ice pack.

Izzy

EIGHTEEN

Dog Days 2005

JULY 14, 2005

THE DOG DAYS HAD OFFICIALLY ARRIVED. IT WAS HOT AND HUMID and the air thick with flies, gnats, and mosquitoes. A muggy mist hung over the farm, and even the animals seemed to be going through the motions. Even Rose grew lethargic about herding, and Orson pretended not to see the chipmunks he usually chased so avidly through the woods.

At five a.m., the sky over the farm was still pitch-black. But in a few minutes, I knew, it would turn gray, and then I'd see a hint of pink in the east, edging the Green Mountains of Vermont. "I think I see Sirius," I said to Orson, but he was already bounding ahead, racing for the ATV.

If I'd learned anything in my years, more than a half century now, it was how predictably the world was filled with unpredictable events and outcomes. The ATV, of all things, had brought me new mobility, and a new bond with Orson.

The hardy little green machine didn't intrude on the natural world; it allowed me to go deeper into it. I loved walking and hoped I'd always walk a few miles each day, but my access to the environment around me had extended only as far as my gimpy legs could take me.

With the ATV, I could go places I couldn't easily reach before, many of them previously unknown to me and quite beautiful. Operated properly, the Kawasaki Prairie chugged up hills, through woods, and down steep trails. Sometimes it hauled loads of hay, firewood, or manure; sometimes its only cargo was a man and a border collie.

It had more effect on Orson than positive reinforcement, herding training, acupuncture, or his Chinese calming herbs. When he bounded out the door, he automatically hopped up onto the rear passenger seat. Clearly, he saw it as his machine.

Often, while up in the pasture or doing chores in the barn, I'd look over to see Orson in his seat, waiting for his chauffeur and our next outing. For a border collie, finding work was no small thing. It had taken us years—and many trainers, vets, behaviorists, communicators, and healers—to find Orson's work. I had no idea that it was purchasable at the Powerline Store in Queensbury. That's what I mean about unpredictability.

Sometimes Orson was so eager for a ride that he sailed right over the seat to the other side. But then he just climbed back up and waited for me. He never fell off when we were moving, though Paula thought I should get him a helmet and seat belt.

He always rode in the same position: behind me, peering straight ahead, his head on my right shoulder. Sometimes, calmer afterward, he would forgo barking at the UPS guy. (But sometimes not.) He barely seemed interested in the sheep any-more. So we were off to greet the Dog Star.

WE CHUGGED UP THROUGH THE PASTURE, A BIT OF AN ADVENTURE even with the headlights on, since the ditches, brush, puddles, and roaming animals were all sometimes hard to distinguish in the darkness. But we rumbled on, over the hill, through a patch of woods, and into a clearing. The youngish trees and remnants of stone fences showed that this had been pasture once, part of a farm years ago. In daylight, you could see across the Black Creek Valley, well into Vermont. At night, because it was the highest point on the farm, we could be close to the heavens.

When I turned off the ATV, the quiet of the forest was thick. Sometimes we saw startled does bounding off. I found a rock to sit on and gazed up, looking for Sirius, the Dog Star, as the eastern sky began to gray. Orson sat beside me.

And there it was, right above us.

Just as the online astronomers and star buffs had promised, Sirius was impossible to miss. "Just look up," one of them had e-mailed me, "and you will find it. Or it will find you."

SIRIUS WAS SO BRIGHT THAT THE ROMANS THOUGHT THE EARTH RE-ceived heat from it (the name derives from the Greek for "scorching" or "searing"). And since in summer the Dog Star rises and sets with the sun, the Romans believed that the sultry weather that descended and lingers during this period, from July 3 to August 11, was caused by Sirius and the sun.

It was a measure of my disconnection from nature, I suppose, that I'd never really focused on the brightest star in the sky. But it wasn't hard to distinguish, once I started looking for it. I just followed instructions: Find Orion, the hunter with the three-starred belt, then look south and to the east to find Sirius.

It's luminous, a major "twinkler." I could only imagine how it must have appeared in times past, when no other light could compete with it or dim it. Now that I knew how to find it, I felt oddly proprietary about it, not only because of the dog connection, but because it seemed to be blazing right at Orson and me.

At those moments, when my dogs and I were stargazing, I thought I knew what people felt in bygone times: This was my star, our star, almost close enough to touch if, as the ancients sometimes thought, I could just find a slightly-taller-than-usual ladder.

"Look how lucky we are, pal," I would tell Orson. "We had a star and we didn't know it."

Now that we understood their origin, the Dog Days ought to be a special time at Bedlam Farm, I thought, an annual commemoration and celebration. We would not merely surrender to heat and humidity and laziness, but take stock, measure things, look ahead. The farm absorbed this ritual, along with other more practical ones, like visits from shearers or the arrival of next winter's hay.

Dogs change all the time, and those of us who live closely with them can miss their sometimes rapid evolution, just as it's easy to overlook your kid growing taller hourly.

So the Dog Days would become a private sort of annual dog festival, when we marked the passage of another year together.

. . .

JULY 5, 2006

IF MY ANIMALS HAVE TAUGHT ME ANYTHING, IT'S THAT LIFE MOVES along its own path, caring little about what we want or how we feel. Perhaps this is why dogs and other animals are so adaptable and stoic, why they seem to accept their fates while we humans struggle so bitterly to alter ours.

Just a year later, in the Dog Days of another summer, Orson is dead. Grass and clover have finally grown over the sandy spots around his grave, with its simple fieldstone marker. Sometimes, when there's a break in the heat, I walk up to visit it.

But Lesley Nase, an animal communicator and shaman I've come to know, says Orson's spirit has left the woods atop the pasture, which he inhabited after his death. He will come to me if I need him, she says, but he has left me and the farm behind, perhaps to enter the lives of other humans.

Now it's usually Izzy who motors up into the woods with me to pay early-morning respects to Sirius. Izzy is different from Orson, not so anxious or so restless. He runs alongside the ATV instead of riding on it, and when we reach the clearing, he very quietly lies beside me, still for as long as I am. It's beautiful to sit with him in the woods, too, while the Dog Star rises with the sun above our valley.

Some of us are here, and some of us are gone, but the Dog Days are back, timeless, greater than us and our insignificant lives, very different and very much the same.

NINETEEN

Dog Days Diaries 2006

I understand why the Romans blamed Sirius, the Dog Star, for the great heat of July and August. Somebody needs to be held responsible.

On these long, sweaty days, my animals slow down, move less, become markedly more nocturnal. The sheep and donkeys graze in the early-morning cool, then hole up in barns and under trees for most of the day. The ewes do not come into breeding season until the weather turns cooler, so Rupert the ram remains fairly affable and hangs around with the donkeys. Elvis and Luna climb up to the top of the hill early in the day and lie down in the shade, nestled together like lovebirds, quite still.

The bugs plague us all. Clouds of mosquitoes swarm around any exposed flesh; billions of gnats fly into your eyes and up your nose. The flies are awful, clustering around animals' eyes, tormenting them. The big horseflies are especially vicious and vampiric; I'm often covered with the welts they leave.

Annie and I diligently apply sprays and creams to try to reduce the attacks. We even put nylon mesh fly masks on the donkeys, although they helpfully pull them off one another within a day or two.

What can you do? Insects, along with a blistering sun on woolly coats and thick hides, seem to be the lot of farm animals, who accept discomfort more readily than I do. The Dog Days are part of their natural cycles, and they simply adapt, as they do to almost everything.

Mother rarely ventures out of the barn during the day, though in the morning she leaves dead things by the side door, perhaps to let me know she's on the case. The chickens scratch out cool holes in the dirt to crawl into, and Winston is rarely heard after six a.m. or so.

This year's cycle seems especially intense. The sun withers the grass and flowers; things have begun to brown and yellow, and the gardens sag. The effect, with so little activity, is almost eerie. Things pick up a bit after dark, with owls hooting and bats out and about. Crickets chirp. I hear a coyote now and then. That's about it.

There is no resting, of course, for the farmers, who can be seen day and sometimes night in near and distant pastures, cutting hay, harvesting crops, watering cows and livestock, riding around the dusty fields on belching tractors. They endure the sun, the humidity, the bugs, the dirt, always focused. "Did you cut your hay?" they ask each other, almost obsessively. "Did you get your corn in?"

My heart is not into herding in the Dog Days. Our lessons and treks with the sheep come early or very late, and they're perfunctory.

Normally, the sheep make Rose come up and get them. In the Dog Days, they seem eager to get the whole business over with, and come rushing down the hill of their own accord as soon as Rose and I enter the pasture. Whether we're going across the road to pasture or to the training pen, they submit briskly and quickly. Everything is finished by nine a.m., when the dogs and I head into the house and the sheep duck into the pole barn and barely stir until sundown.

Izzy, what breeders call a "heat-sensitive" dog, seems uncomfortable in the bright sun, crawling under bushes or trucks for shade. He'd rather lie by an open window and catch the breeze than gallop across a hot pasture. Pearl turns into a cabbage, moving only to eat and put her big beautiful head on my lap for a scratch. Only Rose seems impervious to the weather, as eager and energetic on a ninety-five-degree Dog Day as she is on a crisp fall afternoon.

I slow down myself. I hate naps, and rarely take them, but as the heat builds, I find myself nodding off in mid-afternoon, getting drowsy and slow, like a slug.

Though the days of great heat are not my favorite time, there are some things I appreciate about them. Maybe it's good to slow down for a while, to wait out the summer and spend more time sitting on the front porch, to conserve oneself. Winter is really just around the corner. We will need all the energy we can save.

JULY 6

ALI WAS GOING AWAY TO A CONFERENCE FOR A FEW DAYS, SO Clementine was coming back for a stay at the farm. I picked her up at Ali's office, and she greeted me with the usual enthusiastic licks and Labrador wriggles. She paused to look back at Ali, seemed puzzled, but willingly trotted out with me, jumped into the car, and curled up and dozed until we got home. She got an enthusiastic greeting from the other dogs, even the usually aloof Rose.

At first, I thought she seemed somewhat anxious, a bit confused, but she quickly settled back into her routine. She reclaimed her spot in my bed and resumed her peerless ball-chasing, charging into the woods not only for her own ball, but often returning with her mouth crammed with everybody else's. She rolled in decaying, malodorous stuff. She raided the barn for the cat's food and the chickens' feed. Her appetite was hearty.

I was happy to have her back. Sad, too. I'd missed Clem, a dog who brightened every place she was. I liked waking up in the morning with her sweet face on my shoulder.

But I didn't regret my decision to share her with Ali, nor did I let myself dwell too much on it. I still didn't feel I could do right by four dogs. And I'd come to believe in their remarkable adaptability. Any emotional wrench was mine, not Clementine's. She seemed to adjust happily to both her homes, something important to remember whenever I slipped into the commonplace mistake of assuming that my dogs think the way I do.

One matter remained before our shared custody became a done deal: I had to tell Pam Leslie, Clem's breeder, about the new arrangement. It was something I'd put off, partly because I wanted to see how Clem fared, partly because I feared Pam's disapproval.

I had enormous respect for the care and ethics she brought to her breeding program. For decades, she'd produced a stream of remarkably grounded, even-tempered, beautiful working and companion dogs. People who knew Pam's dogs could spot them a mile away: They stood out.

It had taken me a long time to pry this puppy out of Pam's kennel, so I knew any decision about Clem was something she wouldn't be casual about. I'd warned Ali about it. Pam cared where her dogs went and what happened to them. She would want to know.

If she objected to our arrangement, I'd have to cancel it after only a few weeks and bring Clem back. I had too much respect for Pam, and faith in her judgment about the fate of her dogs, to argue. Tough and direct, not a person to equivocate or beat around the bush, Pam understood that some people found her blunt manner intimidating. She didn't really care.

Pam was one of those breeders who felt a sense of owner-ship of her dogs throughout their lifetime. Other people were only borrowing them, in her view. She would rightfully con-sider it a serious breach of trust for me to change the living arrangements of a dog without consulting her.

So, with a deep breath, I called, and we talked for a while, catching up.

"Listen, I am trying something with Clem and I just want to make sure you're okay with it," I finally said. "If you're not, I'll stop."

Pam went silent. I told her how Izzy had entered my life with a splash. I hadn't initially intended to keep him, but now, I couldn't give him up. But four dogs were too many to take good care of, I'd found. Izzy seemed needier to me than Clementine, not as happy in as many places, not as adaptable, at least not yet. I'd become his safety zone, the base from which he explored the world.

I told Pam how Clem and Ali had bonded over the course of my many visits to her physical therapy center, that Ali was eager for a canine buddy and had asked all the right questions about finding one. I pointed out Ali's flexible work schedule, her athletic life, her desire for a dog to be alongside everywhere she went—hiking, swimming, playing soccer, gathering with friends, visiting her family.

Meanwhile, I went on, my life was getting more frantic. There were more visitors, calls, e-mails, meetings. The border collies had natural work to do, and Pearl, to protect her legs, was constrained in her activities. But Clementine, intensely social and eager to come along, a strong and very athletic dog, might not be getting her due.

She'd been fine, I added hastily. She wasn't being neglected. Yet I was often doing things she couldn't do—herding the sheep, training with Izzy, traveling. She didn't like being left behind, and increasingly, I was leaving her behind.

I told Pam that I believed it my responsibility to give a dog the best possible life, one that allowed the dog to have its fullest potential, not simply to hang on because the dog seemed okay and because conventional wisdom suggested dogs could never, ever be let go, no matter what.

This was not my philosophy. In fact, I thought this increasingly intense view of dogs often kept them from better lives. My border collie Homer was much better suited to being a young family's "only" dog, one who didn't have to compete for attention or negotiate canine politics.

I knew countless dogs—barkers, biters, herders—who would have done far better in environments different from those they were in. But their owners considered it heresy to part with them.

Ali's, I told Pam, was a better home. Clem was getting more attention, more exercise; she got to form the special attachment an only dog feels when it is at the epicenter of a human life and truly shares it. Those were beautiful partnerships, and that was what I sought for Clementine.

A part of me wanted Pam to let me have it and order me to take Clem back, because a part of me wanted her back. The larger part of me, though, honestly believed that this was as good a life as Clem could have.

Pam was quiet for a moment. She didn't seem particularly surprised. She knew about Izzy and probably figured that something would change; she also knew well how easygoing Clementine was.

"Good" was what she said, taking me aback. "This tells me you are growing up as a dog owner and a dog lover. You can let go, in the best interests of the dog. Lots of people can't.

"I know how much you love Clem, because I've seen you two together, many times. This isn't about love, it's about what's best for the dog. So, good for you. Good for her, too."

I was relieved, and I also got the message Pam was sending in her not so subtle way: I'd had some growing up to do. Managing the emotions we feel for the dogs we love never really stops.

Breeders, competitors, and rescue people send dogs away all of the time, of course; it's normal to them. Pet owners don't. It wasn't something I wanted to do often. I'd had some anxiety over my decision to hold on to Izzy, fearing that something would have to give.

Yet I couldn't fault the way it was turning out. Ali felt enriched—"immeasurably," as she put it—having such a good-natured pal to share her life. It was a busy, outdoorsy life, filled with athleticism and friends. Clem got the attention and activity she craved. I got to have the kind of life with dogs I believed in and wanted, with more time to work with them, train them, establish strong connections, and integrate them into my life.

What I was learning, and what Pam had long known, was that finding a better home for a dog isn't the same thing as giving up on a dog. Quite the opposite.

A week later, I drove Clem back to Ali's with more than a few mixed feelings. Clem had done fine, but it was a rip to see her again and another to bring her back. I couldn't help wondering if it was rough on her, too.

When I dropped her off, she ran back and forth between Ali and me. Having fallen back into the rhythms of my life, Clem walked to the door with me when I left.

When I called later that night to make sure she was all right, Ali said she'd seemed anxious for half an hour or so, and then settled back into her routine, with none of the indicators of canine stress—ears or tail down, lethargy, panting, loss of appetite.

Clem, who heartily enjoyed the life of a Lab wherever it was, took a short hike and a swim with Ali, played with the neighbor's dogs, and by eight p.m. was asleep on the couch.

It was great that she and Ali were so happy, that Pam had understood, that I had a solid rationale for what I'd done.

Yet I also felt I had to face a truth, or at least try. I think I know now that my life with dogs may never follow the classic American version.

I hope to have Izzy, Pearl, and Rose forever—it is hard to imagine better, more fitting, more loving and loved companions. But I no longer tell people, the way I used to, that these are the last dogs I will ever own. To do that is to deny the reality of my life, including the limitations caused by my spinal troubles. There may, someday, be other dogs. I suppose there may also, someday, be no dogs.

I felt a growing sorrow after I brought Clem back to Ali's. I hoped to see Clem often during the coming months, but I knew her visits to the farm were likely to become fewer and further apart. Ultimately, she would be somebody else's dog.

JULY 12

I HAD TO GO TO NEW JERSEY FOR SEVERAL DAYS, AND I WANTED TO take Izzy.

He'd been with me for several months now. The dog that had never lived in a house, had bolted when he first glimpsed a donkey, had thrown up each time he rode in a car, had evolved, dramatically.

It seemed I had a particular pal again. Izzy wasn't as simple a dog as Pearl, as focused as Rose, or as easygoing as Clem, but he'd become my partner.

He'd never seen any place like New Jersey, though.

My heart was on the farm, along with my work life, but I'd come to like driving south occasionally, to be with Paula when she couldn't come up, see a few movies, enjoy Thai and Mexican and Japanese restaurants, all in short supply in Washington County. If Izzy was going to be my sidekick, it didn't seem right that he could never visit New Jersey.

Still, a bad idea, I thought.

He'd never encountered a bus, train, or fire engine. The constant traffic, congestion, noise, and constrictions of the place, where he'd have to be leashed and where there were no meadows or woods in which he could run, were likely to be even more upsetting than a donkey.

I didn't need a border collie freaking out in the suburbs. How would he react to groups of kids? Or bicycles? Strollers? He was only recently housebroken. How would he handle strange dogs and smells? If he did freak, where would I take him?

Annie agreed. "He's fine here, and he'll go crazy there," she said.

Paula concurred. "Not a great plan," she said. "He's never been walked on a leash. He just got used to riding in cars and dumping outside."

But Anthony told me to take him. "He'll be fine," he said, brushing off all discussion.

Lesley Nase, the shaman and animal communicator, happened to call at about that time, so I added her to my poll. "It's really about trusting him, isn't it?" she mused. "Why not give Izzy the chance to earn your trust?"

She had a way of cutting to the chase. I didn't really trust this dog, and for good reason. It isn't always noble to trust an animal, especially in a strange situation. Trust a dog too readily, without proper training, and there is frequently trouble.

When the farm, relatively quiet and safe, was new and strange to Izzy, he had destroyed crates, damaged walls and floors, leaped fences. He'd been impulsive and excitable. Perhaps it was too soon, now that he was steady and comfortable, to introduce a new environment, especially one so different, so challenging.

Yet I felt that Izzy needed to trust me, and vice versa. Normally, I believe that dogs ought not be given the chance to fail, which is why I crate them when I go out. But they also need to be given the opportunity to succeed.

So while common sense suggested it was not a shrewd move, I packed up a few dog supplies and whistled for him. "Yo, truck up!" I called, and he bounded happily into the Blazer.

We drove off, waving to Annie, who would care for Pearl

and Rose and the rest of the crew, and to Anthony, working on the barn.

I opened the window a bit for Izzy and he stuck his nose out and sniffed for a few miles, then curled up on the seat and hardly moved again until we got to Montclair, four hours later.

There, he poked his nose out the window again, taking in the strange sights and smells. He looked at me anxiously a few times—when tractor-trailers thundered by or sirens screamed—but much of his earlier frenetic activity and panic seemed to have evaporated.

We pulled into the driveway in front of our apartment, which Paula had rented after we sold our house, a base for her when she was teaching and working in New York. Izzy jumped out to greet her. A bus whined past, followed by a lumbering garbage truck, and he seemed not to notice.

Once he attached to a human—me—the world seemed to make sense to him. That, at least, was my theory: He felt safe.

A friend of mine, a border collie trainer who lives and works in both Ireland and the United States, had come to the farm recently to visit with me and meet Izzy. I told him I'd been a little puzzled by the sudden evolution of this crazed dog into a docile creature who'd integrated himself almost organically into my life.

Sean said he'd seen it before. "This guy is a true working dog," he said. "Not a working dog the way your Rose is. Working is her whole life, and you are a ticket to that show; she loves you for it, but if I brought her to my farm with my sheep, she'd be happy there, too.

"But some working dogs just need a human to attach to, a shepherd. He didn't have that before you, and now he does. The rest is almost incidental."

Sean reminded me that there are enormous variations

within all breeds, but especially the working breeds. "Watching this guy keep his eye on you," he said, "you can see that you are the sun and the moon to each other."

Pearl, he pointed out, was dozing happily on the carpet at the other end of the house. "You can be elsewhere and the world is a good place for her still," he said. Labs are adaptable in that way; it's a big part of why I love them. I thought of Clementine, and her hour-long transition into Ali's life.

"Not this guy," Sean added. "Meet your new shadow."

Dogs who've been neglected often do better in their new homes than abused ones, he said. "They're blank slates," he explained. "Almost like puppies. Until he attached, your world was strange and terrifying. But once he did, it doesn't really matter where you go or what you do."

This trek was proving Sean right. Izzy seemed to have spent years in New Jersey. He paid attention, listening intently to trucks, staring at the variety of dogs he'd never seen before.

He grew obsessed with the fat, lazy squirrels who sashayed around the town parks. Rural squirrels seem to know that any dog they see will soon be hurtling at them at full speed, so they dash into the woods and scamper up trees. Squirrels in New Jersey, however, have learned that dogs are on leashes, and insolently refuse to take off at the sight of them. Izzy might actually have nabbed one, though I declined to give him that opportunity.

There were other attractions, anyway. Delighted by all the people, Izzy went up to strangers and thrust his nose into their hands. He loved kids, and held still for hugs and pats. He considered trying to herd a stroller, but I intervened.

Fascinated by all the movement, he loved riding shotgun in the car, sticking his head out the window to stare at bikers, joggers, and landscapers.

Hoping to acclimate him further, I walked him across the street to the station as an afternoon commuter train from the city was pulling in. There was a deafening whistle, clanging bells, hissing brakes, blaring loudspeakers, shouting conductors, and a stream of people pouring onto the platform—everything required to madden a border collie except fleece.

Izzy sat upright, ears up, eyes wide, head cocked. He stared at the train, then at me. Three or four commuters stopped and asked if they could pat him; he was delighted. "Beautiful dog," one woman said. "So calm." True. We hung around for the next hour or so, and by the time the third train came in, Izzy was lying at my feet, half asleep, while I sat on a bench and read a book.

This, to me, was trust affirmed, trust rewarded. After a few difficult and anxious months, he'd become comfortable as long as he was with me, and it didn't much matter where. Since Izzy would be at my side for many years to come—so I hoped, though it's become painfully clear to me how entwined love and loss can be—it was a welcome development. Because, truth to tell, he also helped me stay grounded and at ease in surroundings that had become almost as alien to me as to him.

JULY 18

IT MAY SOUND STRANGE, GIVEN THAT ROSE AND I SPEND SO MUCH time together and are so important to each other, but for our first three years here, I didn't really know where she slept.

The centerpiece of Bedlam Farm, its heart, is a sprawling old pre–Civil War farmhouse. The ground floor, anchored on each end by large, bright rooms, has been mostly restored, its floors sanded and refinished, the tall windows repaired, the old-style moldings and panels rebuilt. Most of the upstairs, though, remains an untamed labyrinth of musty bedrooms, unfinished lofts, and antiquated closets.

When Clem is in residence, she always comes upstairs with me and claims space at the foot of the bed; in colder weather, snuggling against whatever human warmth she can detect, she'll fight us for the blankets. Izzy also comes up with me and usually spends the night under the bed. Pearl, whose bad legs have made her wary of the steep stairs, sleeps on her own dog bed in the living room. She could make the climb now but she doesn't know it, and with my bed already somewhat crowded, I'm happy to let her consider it out of reach.

Rose stays downstairs when I come up, and I don't usually see her until the middle of the night, somewhere between three and five a.m. Light as a feather, she chooses that hour to hop up onto the bed, tiptoe discreetly around bodies and dogs, lean over, and lick me gently on the chin or cheek half a dozen times. Then she just as lightly sails off and disappears into the recesses of the old house.

But late last night, a fierce thunderstorm struck. The lightning came fast, illuminating the hillsides and pastures all around the house; the thunder cracked and banged and rattled the windows. Border collies are sensitive to loud sounds and vibrations; I knew Rose hated thunder. I soon heard a faint whimpering from somewhere upstairs. Rosie darted anxiously onto the bed, and I felt her tremble. Then another boom hit, and she vanished.

I got up to follow her. She wasn't in Paula's office or in the empty room at the top of the stairs. But when I groped my way into the dank spare bedroom—I'd only been in it a couple of times—lightning brightened the room and I saw Rose curled on the single bed. I'd stumbled onto her lair, I realized, her bat cave. From the bed, you could look out at the pasture and see the sheep, and from the slight indentation on the old quilt, I gathered she'd been doing exactly that.

Two or three rawhide bones lay scattered about along with, to my surprise, two or three of the stuffed animals that the Labs loved to march around with, and which Rose rarely deigned to notice. Privately, though, she'd been assembling a stash of bones and toys, along with two of my socks and a handkerchief. I half expected a bottle of whiskey and a nightstand photo of an old flame.

Rose traveled alone. She was so intense, worked so hard, and kept busy so much of the time that she—just like me—needed a peaceful place all her own. She rarely came up here during the day—she stayed close to the door in case we needed to move sheep—but she understood that when I came up to bed, there was no more work to be done. Now that I knew where she came to chill, I would respect her privacy and keep out of her room unless there was trouble.

This room was far down the fixing-up list. There was a guest room downstairs, and many higher priorities, so we'd simply left this room alone with its warped plywood paneling, dusty brown shag carpet, and stained acoustic-tile ceiling. Nobody had done much to it in thirty or forty years.

The storm raged outside, wind driving the rain against the windowpanes. The thunderclaps had grown bone-rattling. In the intermittent flare of lightning, I saw that Rose was still shaking.

"So this is your place," I said. "Rose's lair."

She wagged.

Rose is not a cuddly dog. She prefers to come in and say hello to you—or not—and then leave.

But this night she kept still as I lay down next to her on the narrow bed and stroked her head and back. We lay like that for nearly half an hour, as the lightning flickered and the thunder boomed and the rain became almost torrential.

I knew quite well how much I needed Rose, but it was easy to forget that Rose sometimes needed me.

When the storm ebbed and the ruckus quieted, Rose stopped shaking and took up position at the window. The sheep and donkeys eventually left the shelter of the pole barn to graze before the heat returned. Rose sighed and lay her head down to sleep, back in charge. I went back to my room and left her to hers.

JULY 19

I ALWAYS THOUGHT OF THE STUDIO BARN ACROSS THE ROAD AS AN eyesore, crammed with junk and detritus from years of under-use and neglect.

My other barns, gorgeous old buildings in varying states of decay, were built for farm purposes—sheltering animals, storing feed and equipment. The big barn, which Anthony was still re-building, was a soaring cathedral, devoted to milking cows. The pig barn, where men from town gathered annually to butcher hogs, was small but elegant. The hay barn across the street was also dignified, an essential storage space.

The studio barn, though, had been built in the 1970s as a little appliance repair shop. It didn't soar. It lacked gracious proportions. It also lacked a purpose, and it interfered with our view of the valley. Anthony and I both had visions of bulldozing it.

But Paula argued to keep the studio barn. It was watertight, it had heat, and somebody would need it one day, she argued in her practical way. So the ugly duckling barn, which I'd never loved, got a reprieve. For a while, a friend used it as a wood-working shop.

Bill and Maria Heinrich, who've become close friends, have an unusual joint career: They restore old farmhouses and other historic structures, then sell them and move on to their next project. Like Anthony, they understand many things I don't about windows, joints and joists, grades of lumber. They also have taste; their carefully researched and restored houses and barns are beautiful, inside and out. Perhaps that's partly because Maria is also an artist—a weaver and a sculptor. And one, since they traveled light and moved often, without a workspace.

This summer I asked Maria if she'd like to work in the studio barn, arranging it any way she chose. She thought about it some, then told me she'd be delighted.

She spent days cleaning out bags of junk from years past. She tore down the dirty blinds, cleaned the windows, spackled and painted.

During the hottest of the Dog Days, I saw her pickup parked by the barn, sometimes late into the night. She moved in a wooden loom on one sticky evening, boxes of supplies on another. My dogs went to visit, especially Pearl, who was happy to keep her company. But I'd promised that once she moved in, I wouldn't enter without knocking.

A few days later, when I saw the studio lights on past dusk on a particularly sultry night, Pearl and I brought some iced tea over and knocked. "Come in," Maria called.

The transformation was stunning. This was no longer an empty barn, a dusty workshop, or an appliance store. With the clean windows looking out over the meadow and the walls painted a cool white, it had become an airy artist's studio, spare, simple, and beautiful.

"Nice work," I said finally, after staring a bit. "Glad you're here." We chatted for a while, and then, all too conscious of how interruption can derail your work, I retreated.

She did have one regular visitor, though, Maria later reported. Mother, delighted to have company at night, often dropped by, knocked a bit of yarn about, and napped in the old leather chair before resuming her lethal prowl. "She's a cool cat," Maria said.

Sitting on the porch later that night, staring at her elegant loom set in the front window, I had the happy sense that Bedlam Farm had an artist in residence. Maria had a studio half the creative types in Manhattan would kill for. And the barn was a beautiful old building; only a fool would want to knock it down.

JULY 28

AT FIRST I ATTRIBUTED ROSE'S LETHARGY TO THE HUMIDITY AND heat. Perhaps the Dog Days had finally slowed my indefatigable partner. She was lying by my feet, unusually still, as I checked my e-mail before heading up to bed. But after typing for a few minutes, I looked down to see a widening puddle of blood beneath her and I jumped up in shock.

"Oh, my God," I said, pulling back her long fur and spotting a bloody gash. "What the hell happened to you?" I scurried to the bathroom, got an adhesive pad to press against the wound—Rose lay ominously quiet—and then wrapped it in rolls of gauze to try to stem the bleeding. I cursed myself for not noticing her wound sooner, called the Granville Small Animal Hospital, and left a message for the morning. But the phone rang in minutes.

Jeff Meyer and his wife, Lynn, a veterinary technician, ran this practice with great personal care; here was Lynn returning my call, though it was nearly ten. I told her what had happened, said it could wait until morning. No, bring Rose in, Lynn said. Jeff would meet me at the office.

Border collies are hardy and stoic, but Rose had taken some dreadful thumpings from recalcitrant animals and suffered other injuries in the line of duty. This one looked like an encounter with a sharp rock, perhaps during our brief herding session earlier in the evening when the sun was weakening. She usually rebounded from these hurts in a day or two, but I didn't want to take chances. I lifted her into the car and headed for Granville.

Jeff was waiting for me in the foyer of his darkened office, along with a tech who'd either been working a night shift or had come in. They took Rose and told me to go home; she followed them so meekly I knew she must be in bad shape.

Jeff called two hours later to report he'd checked out, cleaned, and stitched a deep wound beneath her shoulder, that she'd lost a lot of blood and had to rest—really rest—for two weeks.

Thank God for Jeff and his staff. Over the next few days, Rose dexterously removed all her stitches. Jeff countered by sedating and restitching. She pulled those out, too. He finally, in exasperation, grabbed his surgical staple gun and closed the wound that way. Rose was in and out of his office for days, all activity on the farm coming to a halt in the meantime, until he finally pronounced her healed and fit for duty.

I'd gotten to know Jeff because he'd performed cruciate ligament surgery—two times—on Pearl. That she was as relatively healthy and mobile as she was, her legs now full of metal and plastic and nylon, was a tribute to his skill. I'd started taking the other dogs to him, too, and we'd become friends in the process.

Jeff was a gentle, sweet man, a little shy even though he spent all day talking to people. Like me, he was facing an empty nest and, like me, thinking about what the next phase of his life should be like.

I couldn't see him actually retiring; he'd focused his whole adult life on his family and on caring for animals. In fact, he rarely took more than a day or two off. Once or twice a year, one of his techs told me, he snuck away for a day of fishing, and "that's about it for recreation."

But when he could squeeze some time from his insane schedule, I lured him out to dinner. We both looked forward to that, and his staff thanked me for dragging him away from work for a few hours a month.

The Granville Small Animal practice was housed in a modern building and enjoyed the benefit of highly trained assistants and high-tech equipment. But Jeff ran something of an old-fashioned country practice nonetheless.

There are things you see at a rural vet's that you don't see elsewhere. Farmers taking their dogs home to shoot them because they can't afford or don't believe in expensive therapies. A sedated cougar from a backyard petting zoo lying on an examining table. Dirt-poor kids with pet pigs and baby goats. Plus city people, transplants from Albany and beyond, who'd brought city attitudes to Vermont and Washington County.

Jeff's reputation was growing. When I called researchers at the Cornell Veterinary School for help on a column, a senior staff member asked me where I lived. When I told him, he asked if I knew Jeff.

"He's the best dog vet for two hundred miles, you know," he said. "We recommend him all the time. He does some of the best orthopedic work you'll find anywhere." I'd seen many examples of Jeff's competence firsthand by then, but his self-effacing nature was such that I would never have known he did such specialized work, or that people came such distances to see him.

That made his willingness to cut his rates, or even eliminate them, even more striking. When I'd been involved in moving a number of border collies from Florida to safer homes elsewhere, Jeff had offered to examine and treat all the dogs. "Pay me what you can when you can," he said.

I'd come to love his practice. Joanne, the receptionist, rules the place, selling peanut butter crackers and candy bars as a sideline ("in case anybody needs a snack," she explained). She also mops the floors and shovels snow in the winter. And she brooks no nonsense, from me or anybody else.

Jeff knows all the animals he sees, and their owners as well. He struggles to maintain this personal approach, to give all his patients and their humans his full attention, to get detailed explanations about how the animals are, to follow up as they recover. None of this is cost-effective; all of it makes a great difference.

He and Lynn and the rest of the staff understand how intense Rose is, for instance, so they make her medical treatments a form of work: "Let's go, Rose. Let's go get those shots." She picks up on the tone and goes along.

Pearl, the veteran of so many medical campaigns, is greeted as the pro she is. "Perfect Pearl," Joanne or Toni yells when she comes in, and she practically wriggles herself into the ground. Unlike Rose, Pearl needs no directions. She heads right for the surgical suite or, if given a reprieve—"Not this time, girl"—for the examining room, wagging madly. Of all the breeds I know, only a Lab is so viscerally loving, forgiving, and dopey.

Izzy, new to veterinary care, is approached with compassion and affection. The staff drop to their knees, cuddle and scratch him, kiss him on the nose. He is still a bit wary but agreeable, when his first vet visits could so easily have brought nothing but trauma.

When Jeff and I meet for dinner at the Barn, a homey restaurant in Pawlet, Vermont, we talk about people and their animals, but mostly about our struggles to balance our lives.

Jeff has worked hard for years to make his practice so inviting, to keep his diagnostic and surgical skills honed. As a result, he confronts long hours, a growing client list, and the need to hire and expand, just as I am trying to handle a growing number of intrusions and distractions—mostly the result of things I wanted to happen—that threaten the peaceful nature of the farm.

"I want to keep the practice personal," he told me one night. "I want to know my clients, and their animals, and their lives with their animals. But I've also worked hard to stay up on orthopedic surgery. I love it and I'm doing more of it. So for the first time, we're actually having to turn people away. And I'm looking to hire an associate."

He paused and sipped his soda. "So this is what I've been working toward, what I've always wanted. And this is also what I don't want, and I'm not sure how to manage it."

I understood. And I shrugged and drank my own Diet Coke and we talked some more.

JULY 30

A FARMER CAN, AT TIMES, FEEL LIKE SOMETHING OF A KING. EVEN A sort of farmer like me.

When I walk outside in the morning, every creature in my care notices and responds. The sheep move down toward the feeder, hoping for grain; the donkeys bray because they know I often have cookies and carrots in my pockets; the chickens start toward me because I will soon scatter feed around the barnyard. Mother appears from nowhere, meowing for a cuddle and cat food in her bowl; Elvis comes to the gate for his apple. And the dogs prance and chase each other because the day has begun and they love their rituals.

This is not a question of affection, mostly. The animals like me, the dogs and Mother might even love me. But more significant, I am the source of all the things they need—shelter, water, food, care. Nobody knows what goes on inside an animal's mind, but if everyone materializes when I open the back door, hitch up my jeans, fill my pockets, and march out, I'm sure it's because I provide almost everything that matters to them—except, fortunately, sex.

It can go to your head. But not for long.

The farm is far more humbling than elevating. There are always a dozen developments to track and monitor. Take today.

Pearl is limping, perhaps putting too much strain on those titanium-pinned legs. One of my oldest ewes is listless, drifting away from the flock; I suspect she may be dead by nightfall. Maybe the stifling heat has sickened her. Maybe it's just age.

Days of raging thunderstorms and downpours have washed away part of the hillside, weakening several fenceposts and shorting out the electric fence that keeps Elvis and Luna from wandering out onto the road. Whereupon Elvis does, indeed, walk through the fence and onto the road, where he flirts with a town highway department truck as the horrified driver cowers inside the cab. Rose, recovered and now energized by this challenge and my call to action, tears out onto the road, nipping

Elvis in his hindquarters, with no command from me other than "Get that stupid steer!" Rose knows who belongs where.

Elvis is surprised and mildly annoyed—a small dog worrying his haunches is like a flea to an elephant—but, sensing this little pest's doggedness, he leaves the truck and lumbers up in my direction, snorting and drooling. I whack him on the butt and he clomps back through the gate and doodles up the hill to hang out with Luna. Annie and I get the fence restrung and turned back on, figuring it could have been worse.

And it does get worse; at least, the list of matters demanding attention grows longer. Pearl has waded in one puddle too many and developed a skin infection; I schedule yet another visit to Jeff. Flies are tormenting Rose's still-healing wound and she needs to be sprayed.

Who is really lord of this teeming realm? I learn that a neighbor brush-hogging his meadow with a tractor unknowingly ran over and killed two fawns, and then the mother, who gave her life trying to protect them. I see that hornets have nested, uninvited, on the porch ceiling. Anthony shows up, exhausted from working all day in the heat, to check on me, but who's checking on him? A beam has fallen and grazed his skull, giving him a throbbing headache.

As often as I feel like a VIP, I am quickly brought to my knees. I'm not any sort of monarch. I'm happy just to get through the day.

AUGUST 3

WINSTON CHURCHILL ONCE WROTE THAT SCARCELY ANYTHING THAT he was brought up to believe permanent and vital had lasted, while everything that he was taught was certainly impossible had happened.

I've adopted his words as a sort of motto for life in Bedlam. Scarcely anything I'd expected to happen, or assumed would be lasting, has turned out that way. So many things I'd believed beyond my reach were occurring. It was a bit befuddling.

The Dog Days have turned especially ferocious, setting records for heat, threatening the power grid.

The temperature by the big barn read 104 degrees at 2:30 this afternoon, the highest I've ever seen it rise.

I went outside with the dogs for a brief check on the farm animals, to make sure they had access to fresh water and shade. The sheep were huddled under a tree, and even the arrival of Rose and Izzy stirred no interest; the flock was on strike. Elvis and Luna, way up at the top of the hill, were lying in the shade, motionless except for the occasional ear twitch or swish of a tail. There was no sign of Winston or his hens; they'd undoubtedly found some cooler patch of dirt and dug in.

Mother was batting around a mouse in a desultory way, and then, to my surprise, let the mouse stagger off; she herself slunk into the shaded depths of the barn.

For almost the first time, Rose willingly turned away from the sheep and sat by the back door, wanting to come in. So she was mortal after all.

Pearl made no pretense of wanting to work. On blistering days she merely hustled outside, did her business, and rushed back into the house, taking up position on her back in front of the fan. I checked periodically to make sure she was still alive.

Izzy had been losing patches of fur lately, and Jeff, investigating, had found various mites and parasites in his skin, souvenirs of the years without grooming. He'd been dipped and redipped and then shorn until he looked half his normal size. But he was probably the coolest of us all.

Early this morning, when it was still possible to walk uphill without feeling woozy, I'd made a sorrowful pilgrimage. I went up to Orson's grave site. This day, the last of the Dog Days, was also the anniversary of his death. I sat awhile on the dewy grass, thought of my faithful friend, pictured him loping effortlessly across the pasture. I thought I'd done the right thing, yet to be here without him still felt wrong.

But I couldn't breathe well outside today. The combination of intense heat, humidity, and massive rainfall had stirred my allergies and old bronchial problems and sapped me. I retreated. Now, reassuring myself that my animals were withstanding the day the best they could, I retreated again with Rose, Pearl, and Izzy.

We weren't four distinct beings, these dogs and I, but one unit, happy to be together, living in a kind of affectionate harmony that was a lovely thing for me—a restless and often anxious man—to experience.

We lived in a big house with fans and a couple of air conditioners, thankfully, but we were also an integral part of the farm, and of the farm's organic, timeless stillness. It was beautiful in its own uncomfortable way, and I swore to do justice to it, to protect it. If it ever got cooler.

I'd stashed some damp washcloths in the freezer, and I took out a couple, leaned back on the sofa, and swabbed my sweaty face. Along with the fan, it helped.

It had come to me late in life, this whiff of harmony, and I was enthralled by it and wanted more. I wanted to trust this sense of peace, to turn more of myself over to it. It was an ambitious goal, perhaps my most ambitious, so I was excited about it. I dreaded the day when I stopped hoping for and expecting more.

But I took my cue from my wise animals on that worst of the Dog Day afternoons. I settled down, like them. Izzy jumped onto the couch next to me, and put his head on my lap. He closed his eyes and went to sleep.

So did I.

Restored pig barn

EPILOGUE

THE DOG DAYS HAVE WOUND DOWN. IT'S STILL AUGUST, BUT A slanted light is beginning to creep in, especially in late afternoon, when the sun pales and weakens. The pastures are turning a dustier green; the leaves look tired, pockmarked by the sun and insects. Hot and buggy though the days remain, it's possible to imagine fall, my favorite time of year on the farm.

Outside the kitchen window, I see my wife of more than three decades up in the pasture behind the barn, brushing the donkeys. Lulu and Fanny love the feel of the brush and are on either side, leaning into Paula. Baby Jesus, soon to leave the farm with his mother to take up residence in nearby Cambridge with a young girl who loves them, is behind Paula, nibbling on her pants leg.

Jeannette, irritated that she's not getting priority brushing and food, nips at Paula's knee, as she does when she resents having to share. "Ouch!" I hear Paula object. "Cut it out. You are such a bossy-boots."

I can't say how happy this sight makes me. It was long awaited, hard fought.

Paula brushes the donkeys devotedly, the only farm chore, aside from gathering eggs, she really enjoys. I marvel at how this ferociously independent and work-centered woman, a reporter, professor, and soon an author—I call her the Rose of human beings—is succumbing to the mystical charms of Bedlam Farm. Paula is a native New Yorker and a committed urbanite. She doesn't shovel manure or herd sheep.

But she's come to love the farm. Though not Elvis the steer, undeniably affectionate but so enormous she's afraid one unintended misstep could cripple her forever. Not the sheep, either.

She does love the dogs, and she has great respect for the chickens, who are industrious, consume ticks and other bugs, and produce eggs daily. The only useful creatures on the place, she says. And she loves the donkeys.

A few years earlier, Paula and I went in separate directions on this issue of where to live. I had to get out of New Jersey, for my work and peace of mind. She had to stay, for hers. No matter how many hours we spent shuttling up and down the New York State Thruway, this could have caused real trouble in our marriage. That it hasn't is a miracle, and a tribute to commitment, faith, and understanding.

We understood that we needed and deserved to do what we loved. We decided to support each other by staying close and happily married, while permitting each of us to do what seemed to us essential. We tried to compensate by talking constantly, on the phone, via e-mail, in person, and putting a lot of miles on our cars.

Paula, more than any other human, has supported my life on the farm, even though she didn't particularly want this place, hasn't always approved.

I've worked for years to get her to come to the country, and to make her comfortable here. If I haven't succeeded at the first mission—yet—I may have finally pulled off the second.

Rose was the unwitting inspiration for my get-Paula-to-love-the-farm campaign. I understood that Paula could be reasonably content spending time apart from me, but she couldn't be happy without work.

When I first moved to the farm, Paula set up her desk in the then unrestored Dog Room. But deliverymen, visitors, Anthony and his crew—all had to tromp through the room constantly, as did I whenever I wanted to go outside, get in the car, or walk the dogs.

She could work there, but she wasn't really at ease. It wasn't her space. There was a reason we all called it the Dog Room.

So Anthony carefully restored a spacious unused bedroom upstairs, painting and sanding, putting in new windows and a ceiling fan, exposing the original wooden beams. I spent a small fortune on a computer with the latest satellite Internet connection and a series of signal boosters through the house, so that she could stay in touch with sources, students, friends. Anthony built a big barn-board desk. She has her own phone line.

Upstairs, she can concentrate, free of the distractions, intrusions, and chaos of the farm.

Downstairs, I put a handmade old wing chair in front of the woodstove so she can correct papers, read her beloved *New York Times,* and nitpick my rough chapters in comfort.

It took me a while to get it, but the key to making Paula happy wasn't animal life, or even natural beauty. Just like Rose, she has a strong drive to work.

Now Paula loves to come to the farm, drives up every chance she gets, is happy to take in the view as long as she can also spend some time clicking at the keyboard. She's happy to sit on the front porch, or in her chair by the stove, and read. It's delightful to see her calm down, settle in, and enjoy the infectious peace of the place.

She walks into town each day for exercise or supplies from the Bedlam's Corner Variety Store. She also walks briskly down the wooded trail behind the barn (leaving me behind some-times because I can't walk fast enough). She's made a couple of her own friends, is fulfilling a longtime ambition to learn to cook.

We've remained united while on our different paths, but they're joining together and we seem on the same walkway again, a great joy for me. The farm is a powerful place, and it will have its way with you, which may explain why it is no longer just my place.

On the farm, I've come closer to balance than at any point in my life. I've always found it a struggle to find space for all the elements I want to incorporate into a single existence—spiri-tuality and pragmatism, labor and leisure, quests and stability, love and friendship—and without Paula the struggle might overwhelm me.

Though she never yearned for this place, I couldn't live here a week without her. She helps edit my work, she manages the money and bills, and her love, guidance, and partnership utterly ground me as a human being. Without her, I would float off into space, or fly into confusion, rage, and dysfunction.

AS THE DOG DAYS EBBED, TWO OF MY FAVORITE FEMALES, PAULA AND Pearl, were out on the front porch, catching the early-morning breeze and gazing out over the valley, where farmers were al-ready busily harvesting corn.

Paula was cradling a coffee mug and reading, Pearl beside her, resting her beautiful head on one of Paula's boots.

Of all the things I've witnessed here—death and birth, bru-tal winter and draining summer, the sometimes grueling lives of my neighbors and the dramas of my animals, the lives of the dogs I love—perhaps nothing is as important to me as this scene on the porch.

Stepping back inside the house, I can almost see the parade of life that has led to this moment. I see Orson, the dog who led me here, and Rose, who helps me stay, and the Love Sisters, Pearl and Clem. I can almost hear Anthony high up in the barn rafters, hauling tools and beams up into the air on pulleys.

I see the donkeys standing guard over their sheep, and Mother marauding in the barn. I can picture Izzy running and running along his fence, day after day for three years until we found each other.

And I see this proud, willful woman, my partner in life, finally coming to join me in loving life on this farm, while never surrendering a piece of herself.

What can anyone say at such a moment, but that the monk was right: A life without faith is not possible, and I am, when all is said and done, nothing but a lucky man.

Restored dairy barn

HARMONY AT BEDLAM
by Mary Kellogg

the creek drops to
step dance under the dirt bridge
inviting me
to travel farther
where the farmhouse waits
with its broad welcoming porch

four bounding bodies erupt
Rose, Izzy, Pearl, and Clem
with eager barks of joy
come in, come in

donkeys watch with soulful eyes
begging carrots and back rubs
they lean into me
expectant and confident

calico cat stretches and yawns her contentment
donkey nose sweeps daringly close
she swats it gently

sheep scattered on the hill
munch peacefully
oblivious
border collie Rose, alert to their wandering
herds them toward the gate
Rose rests and watches proudly
her charges safely gathered in

Winston flashes his magnificent comb
and flaunts his plume tail
puffed up and pompous he crows
"I have work to do"

Elvis, bovine, big as a boulder
levels his huge liquid eyes at me
sniffs with his bulbous wet nose
and calmly takes an apple offered

the farm
a portrait of peace
a lesson in tolerance
a network of harmony

July 14, 2006
North Hebron, New York

ACKNOWLEDGMENTS

My wife, Paula Span, has mastered the art of being supportive without necessarily being approving. I'm grateful to her, and to our daughter, Emma, for her great love, friendship, and excellent Yankees blog, eephus.blogspot.com.

Anthony Armstrong, my partner in crime on Bedlam Farm, is like family, along with his wife, Holly, and daughter, Ida. Friendship is, as Emerson said, nature's greatest miracle, and Anthony is one of the blessings of my life.

Wonderful friends are somewhat new to me, and I am grateful for them every day: especially Brian McLendon; Becky MacLachlan; Bill and Maria Heinrich; Rob, Meg, Hunter, and Liz Southerland; and Jeff Meyer.

Annie DiLeo, official Bedlam Farm Goddess, has suffused the farm and its animals with love and trust.

I appreciate my agent, Richard Abate, and my editor, Bruce Tracy, to whom this book is dedicated.

And Dr. Debra Katz of the University of Kentucky, who led me into the rich world of human-animal attachment, and has shaped so much of my work.

Many thanks to Tagalie Heister, a powerful but invisible presence, whose stream of manila envelopes bring not only research but comfort, inspiration, insight, and guidance.

I thank Peter Hanks, whose wonderful pictures bring my words to life, and the other members of his family, with its rich history of progressive farming: Jane and Robin and Dean Hanks.

I am grateful to David Plotz of the online magazine *Slate,* who has firmly and patiently helped teach me how to trust my own stories.

Thanks to Flo Myrick for bringing Izzy into my life, and to Pam Leslie of Hillside Labradors, for producing some of the greatest dogs I've ever known, with the help of Heather Waite.

Nobody runs a farm alone. I thank the staff of the Granville Large Animal Veterinary Service, especially Kirk Ayling and Amanda Alderink. And Ken Norman, friend and farrier, who has always come running to help my donkeys; and Fred De-Paul, legendary Vermont shearer. I am grateful to Ray and Joanne Smith for making me feel so welcome when I first moved upstate and for teaching me so much about sheep and farms.

I'm indebted to my friends and neighbors in the town of Hebron who have befriended me, listened to me, tolerated me.

I'm grateful to George LaVoo, Liz Manne, and Maud Nadler and the staff of HBO Films for making a movie of *A Dog Year* with so much passion and commitment to my story.

Thanks to Don Coldwell for his friendship and wonderful walking sticks. To Nicole Campbell for her unwavering love for animals and people. To Lesley Nase, Bedlam Farm's own shaman, for her insights. To the staffs at the Granville Small Animal Hospital and the Borador Animal Hospital, who take such great care of my dogs.

I thank Joe Donahue, cohost of *Dog Talk* on WAMC, Northeast Public Radio, for his friendship and support.

I thank Margaret Waterson for first encouraging me to write about dogs. Her wisdom and honesty have benefited me and many others.

My dogs, past and present, have brought so many wonderful things to my life.

I will always be grateful to Julius and Stanley, my late faithful companions. I'm particularly thankful for Orson, the dog who really started it all. And for Homer, who accompanied me into the world of sheepherding. I miss Clementine every day, but I'm pleased that she's flourishing and bringing such happiness to her human. Thanks to Pearl for her loving forbearance, to Rose for everything, and to Izzy for deciding to become my dog. We are made for each other.

West Hebron, New York
August 2006

ABOUT THE AUTHOR

Jon Katz has written sixteen books—six novels and ten works of nonfiction—including *A Good Dog, A Dog Year, The Dogs of Bedlam Farm, The New Work of Dogs,* and *Katz on Dogs.* A two-time finalist for the National Magazine Award, he writes columns about dogs and rural life for the online magazine *Slate,* and has written for *The New York Times, The Wall Street Journal, Rolling Stone, GQ,* and the *AKC Gazette.* He cohosts an award-winning show, *Dog Talk,* on Northeast Public Radio. Katz lives on Bedlam Farm in upstate New York with his wife, Paula Span, and his dogs, sheep, steers and cow, donkeys, barn cat, irritable rooster Winston, and three hens. Visit www.bedlamfarm.com.